"Filled with tender encouragement and practical God-centered hope, *Hands Full* is written by a momma who understands. I wish I would have had Brooke's book when my kids were small!"

— JOANNA WEAVER, best-selling author of
Having a Mary Heart in a Martha World

"In these pages, you'll find relatable stories that will help you feel less alone and point your heart back to our only unshakable hope—Jesus Christ. If you love your children and want to embrace the gift of motherhood but sometimes feel like you also want to escape from it, Brooke is the tender and uplifting voice you need on your journey."

— BECKY KEIFE, author of *No Better Mom for the Job*

"Brooke meets moms right in the middle of the messy and grace-filled moments of motherhood and reminds us that God is in the trenches with us. Her humor and humility invite even the busiest and most overwhelmed moms to come sit with Jesus and find refreshment."

— RACHEL DODGE, author of *Praying with Jane: 31 Days Through the Prayers of Jane Austen* and *The Anne of Green Gables Devotional: A Chapter-by-Chapter Companion for Kindred Spirits*

Hands Full

Thirty days of encouragement for busy moms

BROOKE ELLEN FRICK

CrossRiver
ST.JOSEPH, MISSOURI, USA

HANDS FULL
Copyright © 2020 Brooke Ellen Frick

ISBN: 978-1-936501-51-9

For more on Brooke Ellen Frick, visit BrookeFrick.com

Cover design by Carrie Dennis Design
Original package design © 2020 Front cover photo by Jessica Bowers
Author photo by Amy Atkins

Printed in the United States of America

To my Father in Heaven
and to my family here on earth.
Forever grateful for you both.

Contents

Introduction

*I*f you are reading this book right now, it's a miracle. It's a miracle it was published. It's a miracle it was written. And I'm guessing in a smallish sort of way, it's a miracle that you are sitting down reading a book.

Because if there is one thing I know as a mom with my hands full, it is that time is precious and we don't get a lot of it. So, thank you. Thank you for taking some of your valuable time and sharing it with me. As someone who struggles to finish the books I start reading, I do not take that lightly.

The following pages contain a piece of my heart and soul, because they contain my struggles, my failures, my sin, and the grace I keep finding in Jesus Christ. As you will read, I am not a perfect mom. But I'm beyond grateful that I am a forgiven one. And every day, I have a chance to start new with Jesus and my children. I can't ask for anything more.

This little devotional, as I sometimes refer to it, is really not little at all. To me—or to God. It is a dream come true. It is an act of obedience. It has been a process. This book is two-fold evidence to me that first, "God chose the lowly things of this world and the despised things—and the things that are not—to nullify the things that are, so that no one may boast before him," and secondly, that He "is able to do immeasurably more than all we ask or imagine, according to his power that is at work within us" (1 Corinthians 1:28–29, Ephesians 3:20).

I am amazed at His desire to use an ordinary run-of-the-mill mom like me and do more than I could have ever asked. But that is, after all, who He is and what He does. For each of His beloved children.

The stories in this book cover a span of two years because apparently it takes that long for a mom to write a book. I started writing them not knowing they would actually become a book. I just started writing. Writing the things God was revealing to me through some of the hard lessons of living life with my hands overflowing.

So, without further ado, welcome. I am so glad you're here. Pull up a chair, pick up your mug of steaming something, draw the blanket up and be encouraged. You're not the only one with your hands full and your heart in desperate need of Jesus. I hope you find that truth here. I hope you laugh, even if it's very little, because laughter truly is the best medicine, and a happy heart is better than a fine wine or a hot cup of coffee. Mostly, however, I hope you are drawn a little deeper into the depth and breadth of Jesus' love for you. And I pray "you have the power to understand, as all God's people should, how wide, how long, how high, and how deep his love is. May you experience the love of Christ, though it is too great to understand fully. Then you will be made complete with all the fullness of life and power that comes from God" (Ephesians 3:18–19 NLT). May we remember that while our hands may be full, the life inside of us can be even fuller because of the One who loves us, redeems us, and resides in us.

Full Hands or Open Ones

*"Let us then approach God's throne of grace with confidence,
so that we may receive mercy and find grace to help us
in our time of need." Hebrews 4:16*

*I*f I had a dollar for every time I have gotten the comment, "You've got your hands full," I could probably take our family to Disney World.

It's possible I've gotten this comment so much that it has almost become my life motto (if that's even possible) second to my other life motto, "better late than never." Because, seriously, better late than never, right? I'm pretty sure that's even biblical.

Yesterday, I got the hands-full comment from an elderly woman observing us as we strolled around a neighborhood lake: me, an empty double stroller, three tow-headed boys running up ahead and two little girls toddling behind. Today, it was from a dad in the back section of Chick-fil-A by the play area. Same kids, same empty double stroller.

Yes, I've got my hands full, I know. I have five children and two hands. By mathematics alone, my hands are full. I own it. I say yes and smile and carry on as if the entire Chick-fil-A isn't watching, part in wonder, and part in disbelief.

But it isn't easy. Full hands can get heavy. Full hands can feel more than full. They can feel overloaded, overdone, and overwhelmed. It's like comedian Jim Gaffigan said about having four kids. "Just imagine you're drowning—and then someone hands you a baby." I can't think of a better way to describe it.

Drowning. Yes. Life isn't just full; it's like the curbside trash can after Memorial Day weekend: overflowing.

One afternoon a few months ago, I sat in the yellow glider in my girls' room while they pulled torn board books off the shelves and grabbed toys from burlap baskets. I was tired, like usual, and they were happily playing.

They had recently discovered a glass jar on the top shelf filled with little wooden blocks friends had given me at the girls' baby shower. My friends had written sweet little notes in pink and magenta, scribbled designs, and drawn the letters *H* and *R* on them (for my girls' names). They were cute blocks and more for decoration than use, hence the glass jar in a nursery.

But they *loved* pulling these blocks out of this glass jar, and so sometimes I let them. They would stick their plump little hands in, pull them out, and stuff them back in.

That day was a day I let them. They were entertained. For some reason, they began bringing the blocks over to me. I cupped my hands and they started filling them with blocks. With two times the trips, it didn't take long for my hands to become full. With each new load of two or three more blocks, I didn't think I was going to be able to hold any more.

"Uh-oh, my hands are full," I'd say in my exaggerated playful voice. But that didn't deter them. They smiled and kept on bringing the blocks. And so, not wanting to disappoint, I kept trying to hold them. And the amazing thing was I could.

Just when I thought the last block was about to topple, I'd flatten my hands just a little and the blocks would settle in and make room for more. And more. Each time, I'd spread wide my hands and room would be made. I was truly amazed at this anomaly.

I can't count how many times in my motherhood journey I have screamed inside my head, "I can't handle this! No, not the stomach flu while my husband is gone! No, not another sleepless night! No, not lice on Christmas!" (Yep, it happened, and we survived.) My insides are shouting, "There's too much whining, too much bickering, and way more needs than the capacity I have to meet them."

Sometimes I feel like I am a washing machine on a "jumbo wash" cycle and people keep trying to throw more clothes in. "It doesn't fit; I don't have room!" I want to yell.

That's the life of a mother. Maybe that's life in general. Things or people happen that are beyond our control, and what options do we have but to carry on or surrender? Mothers must carry on. But how?

As I sat in my yellow glider that afternoon, God showed me that even when I was sure I couldn't handle any more blocks, I'd stretch out my hands and I would.

By God's magnificent grace, we can handle much much more than we think. And it isn't because we are so strong, or wonderful, or holy, or wise. It's because He is. And when we open wide our hearts, flatten out our expectations, agendas, and perfection, we can say with peace that surpasses understanding, "Okay, Lord, I can't handle this. But you can."

The key is in the letting go, the flattening. In letting Him take over and take the burden.

That day I realized full hands were first open ones. And when we stretch those hands full of blocks or diapers, keys, groceries, and shoes a little wider, with His all-sufficient love and power, we can hold more than we ever thought possible.

PRAYER

Oh God, our lives are full. Our hands overflow with work and life and blessing and so many to-dos. Father, let us come confidently before Your throne of grace to find mercy and grace to help us in our time of need. We bring these burdens to You, these feelings of drowning in a sea of little people and their needs. But You stand ready to help. You are with us and You never forsake us. May we have eyes to see You with. May we lift these full hands to You, flattening our hearts before You, and lay down these things at Your throne, knowing that You will take our burdens upon You. We are not alone. And with Your mercy, grace, and help, You will make a way for us. Amen.

In my Mom Skin

*"Pay careful attention to your own work, for then you
will get the satisfaction of a job well done, and you won't
need to compare yourself to anyone else. For we are each
responsible for our own conduct." Galatians 6:4–5 NLT*

He sat at a low gray table in his tiny navy-blue plastic chair, eating his prepackaged sandwich. Five other little brown, blonde, and black heads sat neatly around his table munching on their lunches, too. More little heads sat at the next table. The room was large and spacious and every wall was covered with an array of bulletin boards, chalkboards, letters of the alphabet, days of the week, colors, numbers, and preschool artwork.

I had gone to school to pick up my son early because grandma was visiting. I hadn't meant to stay for lunch. But realizing they had just begun, I pulled up my chair to enjoy a rare lunch date with my middle child. It was a sweet gift to be able to watch his cute chubby self quietly eating lunch with his friends. He never eats this quietly at home. He looked so grown up.

He picked up his Uncrustable sandwich and took another bite. Just then I felt a stab of remorse. I hadn't made him a peanut butter and jelly sandwich. Smucker's had. I looked over at the girl seated across from him. She took a bite of her whole wheat pita and dipped it in hummus. She had one of those plastic lunch boxes with the compartments for food like all the healthy people use. Sigh. She had a good mom.

I looked back at Lee's lunch. There was the sandwich, of course, a pre-packaged bag of fishy crackers, a juice box (Honest brand at least) and a piece of saltwater taffy. Hmmmm. The mom guilt started to creep up my blue plastic chair and tingle up my spine. My son's entire lunch was prepackaged and there were no fruits or vegetables in sight—just taffy.

I was quick to rationalize. It was a busy week and grandma and grandpa were in town. I don't always pack his lunch this way. We have those plastic lunch boxes too—we just haven't used them yet. And I thought my way back to confirming that I am in fact, still a good mom, even if I sent him to school with vacuumed-packed bags of food.

It's true, it's not just a rationalization. I am a good mom. Sometimes I am even a great mom! (Of course, other times not so great.) Nobody kisses my kids like I do. Nobody reads to them like me. Nobody else trims their nails or asks about their bowel movements like I do. Nope, nobody loves them like I do.

So why does the mom guilt creep in? Why do we look around and compare our job, or our lunch, to someone else's?

At some point I have to get comfortable in my own skin, mothering like I do, without having to explain it to someone else (or rationalize it in my head at a preschool lunch table). I need to be comfortable with what kind of mom I am, without having to give a list of things I do or don't do trying to prove to some invisible panel of snarky parents, who may or may not even exist, that I actually *am* doing the right things to raise my children.

Galatians 6 reminds us, "to pay careful attention to our own work, for then you will get the satisfaction of a job well done, and *you won't need to compare yourself to anyone else*" (emphasis mine).

If we focus on doing our best, mothering the children God has given us, we will receive the contentment that comes with doing just that. We will have peace knowing we did what we could, and we won't feel the need to compare ourselves to the mom next door. But only if we focus on God and pay attention to our own work.

It's like the "stay in your own lane" and "run at your own pace" things people say. When we look around at what others are doing, it's easy to get sidetracked from what God has called us to do. And when we are sidetracked, we are not doing our best.

Sometimes our best may not feel like it is anywhere in the neighborhood of some kind of good. But if it is all we can do at the moment, then it's okay. Grace upon grace, my friend. If our kids are alive and still love us at the end of the day, then I'd say it was a good one.

Because here's some more good news. There is no clean room, no toothpaste-smear-free sink (for more than one day anyway) and no crumbless car seat (ever). If your hands are full like mine, there is always a Lego stuck in the couch, a sock on the floor, or a crayon in your pocket.

There is no perfect house. No perfect lunch. No perfect mom.

The other day, my second-grade son wore a dirty shirt to school, *and I knew it*. It was too late to change, and frankly, if he wanted to wear a dirty shirt to school then—okay. Sometimes I make him change, and sometimes, whatever. Eventually, he will learn, right?

Maybe some people would think I am a bad mom if they

saw my son wearing a dirty shirt to school. But I'm more certain most people wouldn't even notice. And if they do, oh well. At least I'm not the one wearing it. (On second thought, I am probably wearing one, too—with two two-year-olds, my shirts are rarely stainless.)

It is a good feeling getting comfortable in my mom-skin. I pray we all can get here and stay. Because there is never a reason to doubt your mom-ness. I know I don't know you, but I know this: you love your kids and you are doing your very best! You are. Accept it. Own it. Drink it down deep because you and I need to know this.

If we love our kids and try our very best to teach them about Jesus's love for them, then we are good moms--Uncrustable sandwiches and all.

PRAYER

Dear Lord, take away the need we have to compare and contrast ourselves with the moms we know, or the moms we see walking to school and shopping at Target. Help us to fix our eyes on You, who You say we are, and the job You have set before us. Help us to see ourselves as You do: loved and beloved works in progress. Remind us today of Your great love for us and the unique purpose You have given us in raising our little ones. You have entrusted them to us; may we entrust the whole process to You. In Your holy and loving name, we pray. Amen.

In the Strength We Have

"The LORD turned to him and said, 'Go in the strength you have and save Israel out of Midian's hand. Am I not sending you?'" Judges 6:14-15a

Go in the strength you have."

This is the story of Gideon. And I. Love. This. Story. I love how God works in this story. I love how Gideon responds. I love the outcome. I love the drama. I love it all. So, if it has been a while since you've read the story of Gideon, you really need to read it. The whole thing. Beginning to end. Because it is just that good. God is just that good. It's good. Did I already say that? You can find it in Judges 6–7. In fact, I encourage you to put this book down, pull your Bible up on your lap, and read it now. I said, now, (using my mom voice).

(I'll wait while you read…)

Okay, amazing, right? So good.

But in case you're a heathen and didn't read it (just kidding, moms), I will give you a really quick inferior synopsis. Good?

19

Here goes…God calls Gideon to defeat the Midianites, an enemy of Israel who had been raiding and pillaging them. Gideon says, "who, me?" And God says, "Yes, you." (And then they all guess who stole the cookie from the cookie jar). Okay, not really. This is getting out of hand.

Anyway, Gideon is weak and insignificant and sure that God can't be calling him. He questions God. He tests God with fleeces, (I'm sure you have heard about these) and after God "passes" Gideon's tests, Gideon finally believes God is behind him, so he gathers a large army to defeat the Midianites, just like God told him to do. But God thinks Gideon's army is too big, and if this big army defeats the Midianites, God knows they will boast in their own strength and not His. So God shrinks the Israelite army. By *a lot*. And so, with their shrunken army and their unrestricted, ample, all-knowing God, Israel defeats their enemy! Hooray!!

Although there are many amazing take-aways from this story, (that is why you should read it) the thing that has grabbed ahold of me recently is that God didn't fill Gideon with His Spirit when He called him. He filled Gideon once he obeyed and gathered the army to battle the Midianites (Judges 6:34).

When God called Gideon, He told him to "go in the strength" he had. That was it. He didn't tell him to wait until he felt strong enough. He just told him to go. Obey. And even though Gideon had lots of questions and asked for signs (which God graciously provided), Gideon listened. He obeyed.

God is teaching me that it is not about getting the strength we need before we head out on the journey. It's about trusting God and going on it anyway. It's about going in the strength we have now, today, at this moment, not waiting for some supernatural power before we attempt the "impossible."

God wants us to obey Him when He calls, knowing that even

though our resources are so very limited, God's are so very not.

But like Gideon, I question God. "Pardon me, my Lord," but do You know who I am? Did You really call me? Did You really open the door for me to write a devotional? Remember me, the dreamer, not the doer? Did You really mean to give me twins? Remember me, the neat freak, the one who loves order? Me, the fearful one, have You really called me to step out in faith?

The answer is a resounding "Yes!" God is telling me, and He is telling you, dear sister with your hands overflowing to—Go in the strength you have now, because I am going to show you *My* strength.

Go in your strength, because I have infinite strength. Because the fact that you lack strength, actually brings Me more glory. Because when you are weak, I am strong.

I love these lines from Paul, "But he said to me, 'My grace is sufficient for you, for my power is made perfect in weakness.' Therefore, I will boast all the more gladly about my weaknesses, so that Christ's power may rest on me." (2 Corinthians 12: 9).

Our insecurities, weaknesses, and faults do not stop God from calling us. In fact, they may qualify us even more. As Christain pastor and author Mark Batterson so wonderfully puts it, "God doesn't call the qualified, He qualifies the called."

The story of Gideon is certainly one of God qualifying the called. Of God coming through in a ridiculous way to bring His Name ridiculous glory and save His ridiculous people. It's a story of God showing His strength in our weakness.

In short, God gets all the glory when we aren't enough and we do it anyway.

And that, my friends, is why He calls the small and insignificant people like you and me to do great things. That is why He tells us, "Go in the strength you have" because it was never about our strength anyway.

So, I want to ask you, what is God calling you to? Where are you feeling weak? Where are you being called but feeling inadequate? Where are you holding back because you "lack the strength"?

You and me, friend, we cannot sit around and wait for God to show up mightily in our lives. (Unless of course this is what God has told you to do). We have to take God at His word when He tells us things. We have to go in faith. In the strength we have, knowing He will do what He said He will. Even when we don't see how.

So my encouragement to you today is to take Gideon as an example and "Go—" because God will most definitely take care of whatever it is He is calling you to, if you will only let Him.

PRAYER

Heavenly Father, I thank you for the examples in the Bible of how You use Your people and work on their behalf. You are so holy and so wise. I thank You that Your power is infinite, so we need not worry. We only need to trust and obey. You take care of the rest. As we go forth today and tomorrow, may we not be afraid of the things You are calling us to do, but may we simply obey. And as we take these simple steps of faith, as we act in obedience to Your call, may Your name be glorified both now and forevermore. Amen.

He Loved First

"We love because he first loved us." 1 John 4:19

few months ago, I had a thought while brushing my teeth. My three youngest were in the bathroom with me as I tried to accomplish the basics of hygiene. It's sweet, and also a tad annoying how they seem to follow me all around the house. Most days I'd like to brush my teeth in peace and pee in quiet. But that's not exactly how it works with three-year-olds.

It works more like this: I go to get a gallon of milk from the fridge in the garage, and two (or sometimes three) little pairs of feet patter after mine. "I'm just getting a gallon of milk," I say. "I'll be right back. You can stay inside." But they don't listen; they come anyway. And by the time they reach the fridge, I'm on my way back inside.

It's hard to have a moment to yourself as a mom of little ones, because wherever you go, there they are. It's why we find ourselves locked in the bathroom/closet/pantry so we can phone a friend or eat a piece of candy they don't know about.

But that day, while sharing the bathroom with three little people, I had a revelation from God. Or at least, a revelation. While I was mumbling things like, "don't touch that, don't stick those in your ears, and okay you can play with that" with a mouth full of foaming white toothpaste, I had a thought, and it was this:

What if we behaved like our kids do when it comes to following God? What if we wanted to be near Him so badly that we followed Him everywhere He went—even when He was doing ordinary things like brushing his teeth or going to cold dingy places like the garage?

Oh, how I wish it were true. As lofty as the thought was (and how things should be), it left me a little deflated because I knew that was not always the case.

Yes, of course, I want to be where God is, where He is working and loving and present.

Until I don't.

Until I am scared, or selfish, or lazy, or human. Truth be told, I am not always itching to read my Bible or pray. I do it, but I don't always want to. There is a difference.

So often in church on Sundays we sing songs back to God about our love for Him. But I don't always feel it. I wish I could conjure up great feelings for God in those moments, but sometimes, I just can't.

The songs that always get me, however, even on the mornings when my heart feels frosty, are the songs that speak of His love for me. Those songs I can always sing truthfully and they bring tears to my eyes, because they are based on God's unchanging nature, not on my ever-changing state of being.

What makes the Gospel the gospel is that it is not about how much we love God, but about how much He loves us. The Good News is not that we want to be with Him wherever He goes, but that He wants to be with us—wherever we go.

So, the picture I want to stick in my mind is not us walking into the garage with God, but Him walking into the garage with us. He goes with us when we brush our teeth or blow dry our hair. He goes with us to the grocery store and baseball practice. Because He wants to. He goes with us to the dark places, the lonely places, and the scary ones. Again, because He wants to.

He wants to be with us so badly that He left the place where He lived, where He was boss (and recognized as such), where He could eat all the chocolate He wanted, never had a head cold, and never had a need to shed a tear, to be born a baby in a world full of temper tantrums, fevers, mosquitos that bite, and garbage cans that overflow. Just to become Immanuel, "God with us."

Then He went one colossal step further and gave up His *life*, dying a torturous, humiliating, unjust death on a cross in front of a crowd, to remove our sin so that He *could be with us forever*.

Jesus came not so that we could spend eternity with Him, but so that He would get to spend eternity with us. Isn't that just a little bit crazy?

Sometimes I get it so backwards, and I think it's all about me. My desire for Him, my dedication to Him, my obedience to Him, my love for Him.

But it's all about Him. All about His desire for me, His dedication to me, His obedience on my behalf and His unfathomable love for me.

I cannot get over what refreshing *Good News* this is! He initiates. He pursues. He loves. And the only reason we love Him is because He did it first.

I know it may take a leap of faith to picture this, but when your children are following you around the house today from the sink to the stove to the bathroom, try to imagine this is just how much God loves you and how desperate He is to be with you always, wherever you go, for all eternity.

It's a pretty amazing image when you think about it. And when we realize just how furiously and completely we are desired, we can't help but feel a deep love for Him in return.

So friend, while you are burdened with dishes and mismatched socks today, if you feel like you're falling short, or feel distant from Him, just remember He. Loves. You. And He will out love you every single day for the rest of your life. Because He is love, and He loved you first.

PRAYER

Jesus, thank You for loving me so incredibly much. I confess I can't even comprehend how much You love me. But You do. Thank You for being the first to love, the first to initiate, and the pursuer of my heart. You are the lover of my soul. You came all the way from heaven to Earth, to redeem my life from the pit. That's how much You love me. There is no place You will not go for me. No mountain too high, no river too wide, nothing You won't overcome to get to me. I cannot thank You enough. As I go about today, help me see this kind of love and believe it in my heart. In the name above all names, the name of Jesus we pray. Amen.

Just Keep Stirring

"Being confident of this, that he who began a good work in you will carry it on to completion until the day of Christ Jesus." Philippians 1:6

A couple years ago, my mom gave me a baby food cookbook from the 1970s that used to be hers. It's totally old school. Every time I read it I picture earthy moms wearing bell bottoms and making "ants on a log" for their children in striped shirts and bowl-cut hairstyles.

It is a short little book, full of simple, easy recipes for making teething biscuits and toddler snacks and doing homemade kitchen crafts with kids. In it, are a few recipes for making playdough.

Now, I am not a crafty mom. In fact, I did some serious soul searching when Pinterest first came out. As I scrolled the pages, I became more and more certain I was doing this motherhood thing wrong because I had no desire (or ability) to make cookie monster cupcakes for my son's birthday party. To my utmost relief, I soon understood, I was not the only one.

But, unfortunately, like all children, my kids love making "art" out of pipe cleaners, cotton balls, and paint. My kids are junior scientists, artists, and chefs. Then there's me—trying desperately to think of what else we could do on a rainy day when cartoons have been exhausted and the kids are bored.

Making playdough, however, is one of the few crafty things we do in our house. I've dog-eared the page and highlighted the recipe because it is a family favorite. From stirring and adding the dye, to squishing and rolling it out, everybody loves it. I have made it at least a dozen times.

The first time I made playdough, however, I was a little unsure as I stared at the gooey mess I was mixing. It looked like a disaster. I wondered if I had the heat too high, or my pan was too thin, or I wasn't stirring enough.

Then I read her words in the recipe, "it will look like a 'globby' mess and you will be sure it's not turning out...but it will."

Her words brought me the reassurance I needed as I stood over the hot saucepan stirring the white "globby mess" of flour, water, salt, and cream of tartar. But the directions said to be patient and keep stirring. So, I did. And to my amazement, it turned out. Just like she said.

Her words make me think of motherhood. I hope raising kids is a lot like making playdough. I'm hoping that while it sometimes looks and feels like a literal hot mess, in the end everything will all turn out okay.

Obviously, I have not crossed the finish line of launching well-adjusted Jesus-loving adult children into the world. Like you, I'm in the hot globby mess part of it.

Right now, most of the messes I deal with are in the house and involve Legos, crayons, cardboard, or playdough. But as they grow, some of the mess is coming out of their mouths, and out of their hearts.

I'm not sure about you, but sometimes my kids look really gooey. I wonder if anything I am teaching them is sinking in. I wonder if they really trust Jesus. I wonder if they have a deep love for one another down in their hearts, instead of angry words thrust like swords (or along with swords).

And if I'm honest, sometimes I look really gooey too. I'm kind of a yeller, especially at bedtime. Neither can I have too many little people talking to me at the same time because my brain starts to explode (and sometimes I do, too). I talk to my kids about handling their own emotions, and sometimes I'm a horrible example of it.

But here's where I find comfort. I am a work in progress, and so are they. We are one giant hot globby mess. But we're not finished.

As my children continue to grow, I want to remember the truth of the globby mess and that is this: just keep stirring. Don't give up. Don't chuck it out because it looks horrible. Be patient. Keep stirring. Trust the author of the recipe. It is supposed to look this way. The pot is not too thin, nor the heat up too high. For dough to become dough, it must be gooey first. It is all a part of the playdough process.

The older I get, the more and more I wonder whether God's goal really is perfection at all, but the process that takes place in our hearts towards it. Life isn't about getting it perfect. It is about persevering through the sticky gelatinous mess of it.

I love how Oswald Chamber says it, "What we call the process, God calls the end."

So just keep stirring. We are works in progress. He began a good work in us, and He will see it through. One day.

And maybe if I keep drawing nearer to Jesus, then my kids will, too. If I continue to apologize when I mishandle a situation; if I keep learning how to love my children well; if I keep praying for the truth of God's Word to sink into the depths of all of our beings, maybe, just maybe my kids will decide to follow Jesus all of their days and grow into well-adjusted humans. Not perfect ones, but whole and forgiven ones.

I can't hang my hat on this truth just yet. The truth that my kids will be sold-out followers of Jesus if I just keep stirring. But I'm hoping that while sometimes my parenting looks like a giant failure, if I don't give up, my kids will learn to trust Him and go from gooey mess to sticky dough. And as they are smashed, squished, rolled, and cut out, they will be molded and shaped into something beautiful.

PRAYER

Heavenly Father, thank you for making us wonderfully complex! Thank You for making us masterpieces. Thank You for not giving up on us when we look like a hot globby mess (which is often, I'm afraid). Thank You for our children, too, who are sticky messes themselves. I pray that we would trust the Author of the recipe, listen to Your instructions, and just keep stirring. Let us not give up but press on instead. May we continue to do the next right thing, even when, especially when, we are not seeing the results we are wanting or expecting to see. Give us faith and perseverance as mothers who desire to raise godly children who will know and love You the rest of their days. Give us an extra dose of Your amazing grace today. In Jesus name, Amen.

Love Is War

"Hear Israel: Today you are going to battle against your enemies. Do not be fainthearted or afraid; do not panic or be terrified by them. For the LORD your God is the one who goes with you to fight for you against your enemies to give you victory." Deuteronomy 20:3–4

I t was Tuesday, and I was that mother with that toddler having that meltdown in the preschool parking lot.

She had been sleeping soundly on her crib-sheet-covered sleep mat when I went to pick up my girls from preschool that afternoon. She did not want to be awake. She wanted to keep sleeping. Of course.

But sleeping wasn't an option as brother and sister waited for her to wipe her tired eyes and stand up. I grabbed her backpack, her purple water bottle and teal lunch box, along with my sunglasses, keys, and phone.

I managed to get her to wear her unicorn backpack and even carry her lunch box, while I packed up the crib sheet and stuffed it in her sister's backpack. I carried her out to the car, holding the hand of my other daughter and my five-year old son tagging along either ahead or behind, I can't remember.

I do, however, remember the battle that waged once the van doors opened. And I'm guessing a few other folks may remember it, too. It was a scene.

You see, I've calculated how long it takes me to drive to the elementary school where I pick up my third and fourth grade boys. I need to be leaving the preschool no later than 1:50 p.m. to make sure my boys aren't the last ones standing on the curb waiting for their mom or sitting in the office.

We don't have time for dilly-dallying—or tantrums.

But Halle didn't want to get in her car seat. She did not want to be buckled. I felt for her, I really did. Who likes being woken from a nap? My attempts to convince her were futile. The calm coaxing, the bribing (or rewards, however you want to put it), all fell flat, none of it was getting to her. It escalated quickly and she went from crying to crazy mode. The mode where you start wondering if your child is in fact demon possessed as their eyes are rolling back in their heads.

Eventually, I had no choice but to roll up my sleeves and dive in. I stood on the edge of the van leaning over her and basically wrestling my screaming and kicking child into her car seat, all while moms and dads walked by holding hands with their skipping kids and watched.

And after struggling and sweating and being thankful I wasn't wearing a skirt while I stood on the edge of my van and wrangled my daughter into her seat, I calmly stepped down and walked over to my own seat behind the wheel. Then I looked over and noticed the title of the song playing through Pandora on the car radio: "Love Is War."

I didn't feel full of love at that particular moment, but I definitely felt like I had just experienced a war. I had been battling the long hard-fought war of toddlerhood. Of motherhood and car seats and melting-down kids. The war of preschool pickup, and naps that are too short.

There are a lot of battles we fight as moms. Battles we fight with our kids. No, they aren't our enemies, though sometimes it can feel that way. Mostly, we fight battles for our kids. We fight for their education, their sleep, and their safety. We fight battles for their health, their teeth, and their brains. Battles of potty-training, of sleep training, of whining, fighting, hitting, and biting. We fight the battle of the vegetables, clean-ish bedrooms, and homework. We fight against the influence of TV shows, video games, and friends we'd rather they not hang out with. We fight against our own sleep deprivation, mom guilt, and the temptation to think we aren't good enough.

The battle wages on. And on. Sometimes it is fierce, and sometimes it is faint, but it is always always there.

I'm learning; however, the important thing is not that we win every single battle, but that we don't give up on the war. It's important that we keep the fight, keep the faith, and finish the race, just like Paul said (2 Timothy 4:7).

There are more significant battles out there than the car seat struggle (although I can't say it isn't hard). There are spiritual battles we fight for ourselves, and we try to fight for our kids. Although none but Jesus can save our children, we don't give up fighting for them and praying for them to know just how much He loves and desires them to trust Him with their hearts and their lives.

Love fights. Love doesn't give up. Even when they are kicking and screaming, love continues to battle on because love knows the fight is worth it. Because the fight isn't against flesh and blood, but against the spiritual forces working against us (Ephesians 6:12).

Yes, it's important to not give up. And it's very important to know we are not alone in the fight. Deuteronomy 20:4 says, "the Lord your God is the one who goes with you to fight for you."

God fights for us. He goes before us. Indeed, He does, every day everywhere. He never gives up. He relentlessly pursues us with all He has and sometimes He has to do what is necessary to win the battle.

I am ever grateful He fights for me. And I know, friend, He fights for you, too. He sees you fighting all the small battles and all the big ones, and He's right alongside you in that minivan, wrestling that child into her car seat, fighting with you and for you, like a good Father does, because sometimes, love is war.

PRAYER

Father, I thank You that You go with us to fight for us. I thank You that we are not alone in this battle-field called motherhood. You are our "ever present help in trouble" (Psalm 46:1). O God, be that help to us today. Whether we are fighting the car seat battle, the homework battle, the vegetable battle, or God forbid, the stomach flu battle, be our ever-present help. Come to our aid, our rescue. Fight for our children, our marriages, our own relationship with You, and may the Truth win and set us free. In Jesus name we pray, amen.

Only for a Little While

"There is a time for everything, and a season for every activity under the heavens:…He has made everything beautiful in its time." Ecclesiastes 3:1, 11

I'm not sure how many times over the past ten years I have collapsed on the couch with a heavy sigh, uttering the words, "it's just a season" to console myself. It probably outnumbers the number of Legos floating around our house.

A season of night waking, a season of screaming, a season of teething, or potty training, or three kids in diapers, or husband's crazy work schedules. Whatever it is, it always feels like it is going to last *forever*.

But it doesn't.

At times, it feels so eternal that it begins to feel insurmountable. Like life will never be the same again. I'm not even sure what that means, because the reality is, life will never be the same again. Life consists of increments of time and time keeps moving forward, keeps changing, whether you're single, married, 2.5 kids or none. Life is made up of seasons: some good, some great, and some really really hard.

Right now, the leaves outside my windows are turning brown. It's officially fall here in California. The crooked valley oaks with their twisting branches are changing from a dusty green to a dusty brown and their leaves are blowing off, covering the ground with a crunchy blanket.

It's getting cooler, which is a welcome change from the 100 degrees we experienced repeatedly this summer. There is actually a chill in the air that warms in the sun. I am pretty sure this will be the weather in heaven. The horizon is clear and the clouds are puffy and white as, a million miles above me, they inch past the tree limbs. And I remember just how much I love fall.

I love the Cinderella pumpkins and burnt orange mums that sit on porches and steps. I love a PSL from Starbucks, apple-scented candles, caramel corn, hayrides, football, and chili. But there's two things I don't like about fall: the sun goes down early, and winter follows.

As a mom of young children, everyone is quick to tell me things like: "cherish it, it goes by faster than you think," and "enjoy every minute," all of which sound wonderful in theory and impossible in practice. Because cherishing is hard to remember when your kids are screaming and there is spilled milk and broken glass on the kitchen floor.

But, as my kids keep growing up month after month, I am learning they are right. It is only a season, and because of that, we should grab all the good from it we can. Bottle up the wet kisses on our cheeks and the stick figure drawings done in marker, because it is only for a little while.

The book of Ecclesiastes isn't one of the most encouraging books in the Bible. It is confusing and even depressing at times. It is hard to understand, and I am the first to admit, I do not comprehend all that we are supposed to glean from this book. One thing, however, I have gleaned from Ecclesiastes is the lesson of seasons.

In Ecclesiastes 3:1 Solomon writes, "There is a time for everything, and a season for every activity under the heavens." He shares about times to mourn and dance, mend and tear, times for war and times for peace. It's beautiful and poetic and true.

In our lives as mothers, there is beauty, truth, and seasons, too. There is a time to nurse, and a time to stop nursing. A time to sleep...and a time to not sleep. A time to change diapers, and time to potty train. A time for being home, and a time for school. A time to bud a tooth and a time to lose one.

When things are hard, it is comforting to know it won't last forever. But what about all the good things that don't last forever? The unexpected hugs while I'm cooking dinner, the dandelion presents, and the way their eyes light up when I give them two nickels.

A few verses later Solomon writes this:

"I have seen the burden God has laid on the human race. He has made everything beautiful in its time. ...That each of them may eat and drink, and find satisfaction in all their toil—this is the gift of God" (10, 11, 13).

God sees. He knows the burden He has given us in raising children. He knows how hard it all is. He knows motherhood is full of toil. It isn't all bad, of course, but it is a lot of work. Feeding, changing, cleaning, driving, laundering, wiping, teaching, guiding, disciplining, and on and on.

But "He has made everything beautiful in its time." Life, though it be full of work, is still beautiful.

It's kind of like God working all things together for the good of those who love Him and are called according to His purpose (Romans 8:28). Even the hard parts of a season are beautiful. It may be a different kind of beauty, and beauty may not unfold until later, but beauty will be found…in time.

Among the burdens of motherhood, we find some remarkable blessings. Blessings that are only given to parents. The blessing of experiencing a love like you never knew existed, the blessing of humility, the blessing of weakness, the blessing of forgiveness, and the blessing of watching life develop in front of our eyeballs. We get to witness their first steps, first words, first tooth, and their first failure.

No, it is not all easy, but it is all beautiful. The macaroni and cheese stained walls, the ink on the family room couch, and the toothpaste ground into the carpet. They are remnants of lives being lived, and children being raised, and it won't last forever. God, give us eyes to see this with. Always.

Let us find the beauty in the season and leave the burden with God. Because the gift of God in the work of motherhood is the joy we find in it. Sometimes we miss childhood for the children. Sometimes we don't realize how blessed we are to be able to sit on our stained couches and read books to our stinky-feet children with toys all over the floor.

God, let us remember that life is eternal, not the season, whether it be delightful or difficult. I want to cherish these full hands. These full days. This full heart. These stained shirts and scribbled walls. Because it is, after all, only for a little while.

And while the days get shorter and the trees outside my window become more and more barren, I'll take joy in the things I love about fall and make the most of the things I don't. And I will remember, God makes all things beautiful in time.

PRAYER

O Father, we thank You for seasons, good ones and hard ones, and we thank You most of all that You make all things beautiful in their time. We can trust You with all things because You are so so good to us. Help us find joy in the season we are in today. Help us to see these children as blessings not burdens. And when things or people feel like a burden, may we hand them over to You and let the burden rest on Your shoulders, while we stay sheltered in Your everlasting arms. And may we remember to see the joy in all things, especially the hard things. Amen.

Grace and the Man on the Airplane

"For from his fullness we have all received, grace upon grace." John 1:16 ESV (emphasis mine)

I'll never forget his words. I had found out five weeks ago I was pregnant with twins. We hadn't told anyone but our parents and two or three others. We were waiting. Waiting to share the most shocking news we've ever received because, well, we wanted to be sure that everything was going to be okay, and we wanted to be excited (and not completely freaked and overwhelmed) when we told them.

We happened to be flying home to see my entire family in Virginia that spring, and we figured it was as good a time as any to let the cat out of the bag.

So we flew there and back on an airplane with our boys, 6, 4, and 18 months, and my belly home to two more children whom we were grateful for, but completely blindsided by.

We had a fun-filled week with family as we shared the news, but we flew back over-tired, adjusted to a different time zone, and ready to be home. It's not a great combination for great behavior in anyone, especially kids.

Our vigorous and high energy boys fought on and off the whole five-hour plane ride home. Sure, they watched their movies, but they also pushed, and argued, and fought over crayons, or coloring books, and who even remembers what else.

I just remember the older couple sitting two rows back. The ones in their seventies, who made comments to themselves loud enough for us to hear. I'm grateful I didn't hear most of what they said or laughed at while my husband tried to quietly reprimand our blossoming boys (or threaten them—you know, whatever works).

But I did hear very clearly one particular comment he said as he laughed and watched us stagger off the plane, our arms heavy with all kinds of blankets and backpacks and unused jackets, and our hearts just as weary.

"Looks like you need another one!" He laughed sarcastically, this time speaking more at us, than about us. He thought it was hilarious.

Part of me wanted to lash out at him, and the other part of me wanted to curl up in a ball and cry. Little did he know, I was thirteen weeks pregnant with twins. God was giving us not just *one* more baby with our already full hands, but *two*.

Instead of doing either, I pretended not to hear him as I held my son, shouldered my purse the size of him, and shuffled off the plane with tears building in my eyes.

I have gotten a lot of comments over my ten years of being a mom, both good and bad, but nothing has stung quite like this one.

Maybe it's because it felt like he was laughing at our situation. Maybe it's because he was being kind of rude, even if he didn't realize it.

Or maybe it's because it pinpointed my own insecurity. We already had our hands full with our three boys, and now we were adding twins into the mix. What was God thinking? How could this be a good idea? How would we do it? I honestly wasn't sure. I knew we were going to need some serious prayer and some serious hands. And his comment came smack dab in the middle of all my own questions about our capacity.

In about six months, we were going to have a first-grade school schedule, a kindergarten school schedule, a two-year-old, and newborn twins. That does not sound like a recipe for how to live your best life.

It hurt because I hurt. And that man didn't know it. He shouldn't have said what he said, but he also didn't know what I was already feeling and what was happening to my body. Perhaps if he had, he would have been quiet.

By this, I'm reminded that so many of us don't know the whole story but feel compelled to speak in anyway.

Maybe the things we say are not as obviously hurtful as the comments we received on the airplane that day, but it reminds me to be careful with my words. To not speak idly, and to forgive others when they do.

As moms with young kids, we get comments. It is, apparently, part of the deal. It's things like this that nobody tells you in birthing class. Although, you figure it out soon enough on your own. But maybe we haven't figured out quite as quickly what to do with these comments. Because once they start, they don't stop.

Best-selling author and motivational speaker Andy Andrews said, "Every single day for the rest of your life, somebody is going to push you in the pool. And you better decide now how you're going to act when it happens." How we ring the water out of our shirts, twist it out of our hair, and walk on makes a difference.

Nothing pushes us in the pool more often than words. Words hurt. Sting. And are remembered for years beyond their delivery.

But we don't have to let them keep us drowning in the pool. Or secretly wanting to push someone else in.

If I am going to survive Target runs with all five children, eating in public, and traveling as a family on an airplane, then I am going to have to figure out how I'll respond when somebody pushes me or my kids in the pool.

I know it seems a little much, but I can't help but think of Jesus' words while he hung dying on the cross for the sins of the world He didn't commit. He said, "Father, forgive them, they do not know what they do" (Luke 23:34 NKJV).

Most of us are the people who don't realize what we do. Sometimes, we don't think before we speak or act. Sometimes we do—and also need forgiveness.

The Bible reminds us to "Bear with each other and forgive one another if any of you has a grievance against someone. Forgive as the Lord forgave you" (Colossians 3:13).

Forgiveness and grace. That is how we survive being pushed in the pool. We give grace to the impulsive loose-lipped strangers our kids bump into, and we give lots of grace to ourselves. We are doing the best we can, even if others don't see it. Our kids are doing the best they can, or at the very least, they are in the middle of growing up. They need time to develop into compassionate, grateful, and respectful people.

The clerk at the grocery store? She is doing the best she can. That man on the airplane? Same thing. There is not a human being on this planet that does not need the forgiveness and grace of Jesus Christ. Let's not forget it. Because it's grace upon grace, my friends, that helps us make it through.

PRAYER

Lord, we thank You for Your forgiveness. Thank You for Your grace and love that covers a multitude of sins (1 Peter 4:8). Forgive us for words we have spoken idly to those we love or those we barely know. Convict our hearts where we need it and keep our lips from speaking unkindness. And God give us grace as we inevitably encounter others who sting us with their words. Give us grace to respond in a loving way, and may we never hold a grudge against a person made in Your image. And if we have, O Lord, sort it out in us and deliver us from the root of bitterness, anger, and unforgiveness. We thank You for this day You have given us. In Your name we pray. Amen.

Feelings Are Real

*"Then you will know the truth, and the
truth will set you free." John 8:32*

*"The heart is deceitful above all things and beyond
cure. Who can understand it?" Jeremiah 17:9*

I hate you!"

I remember the first time I heard those words come from the lips of one of my babes. It was my first born. He was six, and I wouldn't let him go swimming at the neighbor's house. So he stood in the doorway to my room, with red cheeks and blond hair, a mess of tears, and hurled those words at me.

Amazingly, I remained calm as I listened to words for the first time that no mom ever wants to hear. It was shocking; it was hurtful; it was not what I expected to hear after denying a request to swim with friends. But, let's be honest, it was also almost laughable. Hatred. Over not being able to go swimming. Really?

I knew he was upset, but I also knew it wasn't true. And I

found myself almost holding back laughter. I am his mother. I wipe his boogers and help him brush his teeth. I stay up with him at night when he is sick. I make his favorite kind of macaroni and cheese, and he holds my hand when we walk to school. I *know* that one afternoon of denying his heart's desire was not going to change all of that. I love him and he loves me, even if he didn't feel it at that moment.

That afternoon, he was mad and no doubt had some strong feelings of dislike for me. Mostly, however, he was not upset with me, but with the fact that he couldn't swim. His intense feelings were very real. But what wasn't real, was the statement he made. He didn't hate me. I knew it. And it was this knowledge that took the sting out of his words and lessened their threat. It allowed me to react in a calm, positive manner and talk him down from the cliff—eventually.

I was talking to my older sister on the phone the other day and she said some of the wisest words I have heard in a while. It is something she has been learning in her own life, and it was this: "Feelings are real, but they are not true."

A light bulb went off in my head. How many times have I had that conversation with my husband? The one where I say all the things I am feeling, and he tries to speak logic into every single one. "But, noooo," I urge. "I feeeeellll _____." It's hard to argue with another person's feelings, isn't it? It's hard to speak logic to an emotional brain. My husband has become a good listener. But I am also learning—sometimes, he is right.

Yes, feelings are real. They cannot be stuffed or denied or ignored. Feelings need to be felt.

Still, just because they are real (and sometimes powerful), it doesn't make them true. Not always.

As a woman and a mom, I have a lot of feelings. Sometimes I can feel unloved by my husband or left out by friends. I can feel like the boring mom because I don't do crafts or art projects with my children. I can feel like the monster mom when I have disciplined out of anger. I can feel like I don't measure up to some impossible invisible standard of motherhood, or wifehood, or whatever. And I can feel, sometimes, like it's all just too much and there is no way I will ever keep up.

But what I'm starting to learn is that while the feelings themselves cannot be denied, the truth behind them can.

I am loved by my husband. I am valued by my friends. I am adored by my kids. I am a good mom because I love them, imperfectly as it may look. Yes, maybe sometimes, it is all a little too much, and that is why I need Jesus.

Even as I say this, I know while nine times out of ten, our husbands don't mean to hurt our feelings, and our friends don't mean to leave us out, there are times when people *do* intentionally hurt us. That happens. And when it happens, the truth hurts. Badly.

But even in the hurt, whether it's based on truth or not, we can come to Jesus and find a firm undeniable truth: we are accepted and loved right where we are, just as we are, by our Creator. No conditions. No exceptions. We are beyond valuable to Him. We have been rescued. Delivered. Bought back from the one who sought to destroy us. We have gone from a kingdom of darkness to a kingdom of light. Hallelujah! Thank you, Jesus!

If you confess to know Jesus, you can't deny this truth, whether or not you feel it. The Bible repeats it over and over and over.

John 8:32 says, "you will know the truth, and the truth will set you free." He's talking about the truth of Jesus' life and death and resurrection. The gospel. And this gospel, this good news, sets us free. Free from judgement, free from expectation, free from wrath, free from slavery. Free from fear. It's the most liberating freedom in the world.

But in so many smaller ways, undeniable truths in life sets

us free as well. Like the truths that may contradict our feelings. The truth about our kids, our spouses, our girlfriends, and our motherhood.

If we are patient with ourselves and seek truth, we will find it. And when our children speak out in anger against us, or we don't get invited to the birthday party, or our husband forgets to call on an overnight trip, we can begin to decipher the truth from the feeling and be set free.

My son stayed mad at me a good portion of that afternoon, for refusing a swim, but ultimately, he apologized, and we went to bed on good terms. I kissed his forehead as I tucked him in and said a prayer. He kissed me back and wrapped his thin arms around my neck. "I love you," he whispered. I smiled and kissed him again. I knew this time his words were true ones.

PRAYER

Heavenly Father, thank You for emotions and the ability to feel all different kinds. Although they are not always pleasant, they can be used to drive us back to You by our human inadequacies. We thank You most of all that there is Truth. Help us to see this Truth today where our vision is blurry or our hearts are wounded. God, You are the Truth. You are the Rescuer and Redeemer of our lives. You have set us free and we cannot thank You enough for that. God, go with us today and dispel the lies we are tempted to believe. Point out the errors of our thinking and replace it with the Truth of Your Word. In Jesus name we pray, Amen.

Broken Cisterns

"My people have committed two sins: They have forsaken me,
the spring of living water, and have dug their own cisterns,
broken cisterns that cannot hold water." Jeremiah 2:13

We live in the country, which means we live on a well. Because our particular well isn't a very good one, and only pumps a few gallons a minute (equate a trickle from the faucet), someone built a storage tank, or a cistern, to hold water from our well so that more than a trickle comes out when we wash dishes, and bathe, and all of the things that involve water. It works pretty well, until suddenly it doesn't.

This spring, we put in a rectangle of sod and a sprinkler system, so that when everything else goes brown this summer, we will have a patch of cool green grass for the kids to play on.

Well, yesterday, that sprinkler system got a leak. A big one. So big in fact, it drained our cistern. The really unfortunate part is once our tank drains, we run out of water for hours (sometimes twenty-four) until it has time to fill back up. It becomes an empty cistern.

I read this verse several months ago, and my soul caught in my throat. Probably because without even fully knowing what a cistern was, I was pretty sure I was digging one. And not only was I digging one, it was also leaking.

Still, not until this past week, did I have tangible example of the ramifications of relying on a cistern for water, as opposed to a well.

I'm sure you get it by now, but a cistern is basically a storage tank for holding water. In Bible times, a cistern was mostly used to capture rain and other runoff water and store it for use. It differs from a well in that it does not tap into underground springs. A cistern will always eventually run dry; wells don't, or at least they shouldn't.

"My people have committed two sins," God says in Jeremiah 2:13. "They have forsaken me, the spring of living water, and have dug their own cisterns, broken cisterns that cannot hold water."

Of course, this is all metaphorical. Whether or not they were really digging cisterns, I do not know. But I do know God was more concerned with the condition of their hearts than the source of their water. They forsook the true source of Living Water, the power of God, to build their own broken source of life.

It seems to me that a cistern is the lazy man's well. Cisterns let us catch all the runoff and rainwater without having to do the hard work of digging down deep to tap into the ultimate source of water.

If I'm honest, I do that a lot in life. I listen to worship music, I read an inspiring Christian book or a few words in a devotional and plan on that filling my tank. But sometimes, all I am doing is catching the runoff. Catching the runoff of other people's experiences with Jesus, instead of developing my own.

Instead of soul-searching with God and letting Him dig up the deep parts of me to get at the Source, I dig my own cistern.

It's filled with a few verses and quotes, a good conversation about God with a friend, lyrics from a song, or a powerful sermon from Sunday. These are all great things; they are water to my soul. But the water doesn't last long because it is not the Source. Only Jesus is that.

Not only is my storage tank sometimes disconnected from the everlasting Source, it is broken. My cistern is cracked, and so it leaks. A little bit here, a little there. And if the sprinkler system breaks, or someone leaves a hose on, the leak becomes a gush and pretty soon, I'm drained. As a mom, it often feels like all of the faucets are attached to me. The days filled with whining, meltdowns, and a million spills feel a lot like someone left the kitchen faucet on all day. Those days are draining, and I am continually leaking water, just like our storage tank.

But the beauty of staying connected to the Source is, we will not be emptying our own resources and so won't run dry. As followers of Christ, we have the amazing opportunity to daily pull up our water, our source of life, from Him. The energy, patience, love, grace, and forgiveness for my husband, my kids, my relatives, don't have to come from my own shallow waters. They can come from His. Isn't that wonderful news?

I want to be more of a well, and less of a cistern. Not living out of the stored-up waters, but continually connected to the everlasting underground Source of water and life. Because on my own I am shallow and broken and leaking. But with God, I am deep, and whole, and sealed. And that, my mom friends, is a much better way to live, because when somebody leaves the hose on, there will still be water to spare. For now until forever. Amen.

PRAYER

God forgive us for forsaking You and trying to dig our own cisterns, be our own saviors and our own source of life. We cannot do it. We were not made to. We are weak and frail and prone to sin. Our cisterns will always leak. But You are the Source of Life. The only One who never runs dry, and if we drink the water from Your well, we will never thirst again (John 4:14). O Father, may we be connected to this Source. May we drink this water day after day and out of us will flow rivers of living water (John 7:37–38). May it be so. Amen!

But here I am, writing a devotional

"For God, who said, 'Let light shine out of darkness,'...But we have this treasure in jars of clay to show that this all-surpassing power belongs to God and not to us." 2 Corinthians 4:6-7

Friends, I'm gonna be honest here and hope you keep reading. I feel like the least likely candidate to be writing a devotional.

Me. The little stay-at-home mom whose kids wear the same socks day after day, and whose van is full of crunched cheerios and soggy fries. The mom who loses her cool around bedtime and forgets to read her Bible. Me? Devotional?

I thought only super holy people wrote those. People who have it all figured out. They are the ones who write about Jesus. People who sit for hours and hours at His feet, listening, praying, reading their Bibles day and night. They are the devotional writers. Not regular people like me.

I love my Jesus, I do. But sometimes I am so lousy at showing it. At doing it. And I can think of women I know who seem a lot more qualified to be writing this book than me.

Yet here I am, sitting in a drafty coffee shop at a teetering table with cold ankles, using my few kid-free hours to write a devotional. Why?

Because I need Jesus, and God must like that.

Because one thing the Bible continually teaches me is that God loves to use the weak things of this world to bring Himself glory. Because when we are weak, He is strong (2 Cor. 12:10). Because our treasure—Jesus—lives in simple jars of clay, like us, to show that this glory is not our own (2 Cor. 5:6–7).

Because perfection or righteousness is not a prerequisite for God's love to shine through us. This is great news for humanity, because if that is the case, everybody qualifies to be loved and used by God.

So, I sit here and write, not because I am holy, but because He is. And when you say yes to God, He does some pretty crazy things.

The only reason, I am writing today is because I let go of my fears and feelings of inadequacy and decided to follow where Jesus was leading me in faith and obedience. I finally believed Him more than my fears. And I knew that God had put desires and gifts in my heart He wanted me to unwrap, to feel, and to use.

I'm writing a devotional because God is good and so, so gracious. Because as far as the east is from the west, He has removed my selfishness, my negative thoughts, my lack of discipline, and my feelings of inadequacy from me (Psalm 103:12).

For too long I have let fears and my shortcomings speake louder than Jesus. My fear of the hard things that come with stepping out in faith. The fear of what others may think. The fear of negative feedback. The fear of the trials I might undergo as a result of following Him.

For too long I have let these lies speak louder than the truth. The truth that I am wholly and dearly loved, in the midst of it all. The truth that He still wants me as His daughter and calls me to share His glory, knowing full well, I don't have it all figured out.

The truth the Bible tells me is that I am not supposed to be a crystal vase, but instead a jar of clay: an ordinary, common-place, functional jar filled with a glory that isn't my own.

Friend, don't let your jar of clay keep you from feeling you can't shine the light of Jesus. Don't let your fears or your shortcomings speak louder than Jesus. He loves all of you. He wants all of you. And all He requires is that you trust Him and follow His lead.

As I walk this mom journey, I am trying to lean into the lessons God is teaching me. And one is this: God loves using ordinary people to shine His glory.

So maybe, after all, I am a fitting person to be writing a de-votional for moms, because my failings will point you to Jesus and not to me. Because maybe all God really wants of me is to be available, not perfect. Maybe He desires my obedience over my righteousness. Maybe God wants the same from you.

Friends, you don't have to be perfect to be used by God and raise your children. Not even close, because it's not even possible. You are a jar of clay. A beautiful, ordinary jar of clay filled with an extraordinary treasure that is not our own. And He wants to use you right where you are.

PRAYER

God, thank you for using ordinary people like me and your daughters who are reading this book. Thank You for choosing to fill us, these simple jars of clay, with Your unfathomable glory. Thank You for loving us despite our sin and brokenness. And God, I ask for boldness today. Boldness in knowing who we are in You and stepping out in faith and obedience to do the very things we feel You calling us toward but too weak to do. Remind us that even if we don't feel worthy, You call us worthy because we have trusted in Jesus Christ's sacrifice for us. Without You, we are nothing, but in You we have everything because Your Spirit dwells within us. What an amazing thing! With that knowledge may we let go of our fears today. May we let go of those things that keep us from showing Your glory and live lives worthy of the calling of Christ (Ephesians 4:1).

Functioning in Chaos

"If you wait for perfect conditions; you will never get anything done." Ecclesiastes 11:4 TLB

I am a bit of a control freak. When someone gets the stomach flu in my house, I break out the Lysol like it's my full-time job, wiping down everything from light switches to cabinet pulls to remotes and board books. It's my attempt to control the situation. It may be an illusion of power, but it helps my little brain.

However, like the stomach flu, motherhood is full of the uncontrollable and the unexpected. And I've come to realize through this sanctifying process, that it's not just motherhood that is uncontrollable and unexpected, it's life.

Perhaps when I was single, or newly married, life didn't seem quite so unpredictable. That didn't mean it wasn't; I just didn't see it that way as often as I do now.

Now, as a mother of five, including the unexpected gift of spontaneous identical twins, there is no doubt in my mind that my life is out of my hands, and I live in a chaotic uncontrollable world.

That's the bad news. The good news is my life is in God's hands, and that is a much safer place to be than mine. Scarier? Maybe. Safer? Absolutely!

But back to the chaos. Chaos is the essence of motherhood. Anarchy versus order. Clean versus clutter. These—and many others—are the battles we fight.

Before I sat down to write this, I had to step over fifty puzzle pieces to get to my desk. Twenty-two alphabet blocks, a blue plastic football from All-State Insurance, a backpack, some Wild Kratts toys and a Little Tikes vacuum round out the pile. Basically, somebody dumped out one of the cute little bins full of toys sitting on the shelf, and it's now a trash pile of toys through which I must wade to get to my desk.

So here I am, sitting and writing in the middle of it. That's kinda how life feels right now, like I'm I the middle of a trash pile of toys. (Maybe that's because I am.) I am surrounded daily by all kinds of crazy. I know you are, too.

As moms, our lives are filled with pandemonium, and somehow, in the middle of it, we are called to make peanut butter and jelly sandwiches, swath Neosporin over a boo-boo, cook the family meal, teach our children how to handle their emotions, pay the water bill, and keep our marriages alive and well. We are called to function from the middle of craziness. And it. Is. Haaaarrrrdddd.

At some point along the way of my motherhood journey, I realized I couldn't control the clutter, the chaos, or the crumbs, so I started functioning in the middle of it; despite it.

So now I sit at my desk (I know I'm lucky to even have one) and write in the middle of a room full of toys. Forsaking the temporary for the eternal.

And I'm thinking, this is the sweet spot.

I've been telling my friends lately that I am a better mom

to five kids than I was to one. Alright, in many ways that's not a fair statement.

When I start to think about it practically, it's not true. We eat more Chick-fil-A and pizza than we should, bathe much less often than we used to, and my boys almost always have dirt in their fingernails. And everyone needs a haircut. Like always. I don't read books with them as often as I used to, and dishes are continually found in the sink. I missed two years of my middle son's well visits!

But the reason, I beg to argue, that I am a better mom to five than one, is because my underwear is much less bundled than it used to be.

I've relaxed. Like, a lot. Because when you have five kids and only two hands, you don't have a choice. Because when I walk from the van full of wet beach towels, snacks, trash, and sunscreen, into a kitchen that hasn't been cleaned since last night and everyone is "starving" for lunch, I do what needs to be done and let go of the rest. Because I can't do it all. Because I'm outnumbered and as hard as I try, I'm just not super mom.

My sharp edges, my perfectionist tendencies, my control-freakiness are all being smoothed over. Jesus is transforming me daily through the chaos. It's hard, but it is oh so good.

God is teaching me that a big part of life is just figuring out what is important and what isn't. Trash in the minivan isn't important. Not really. It only gets important when the cheeseburger mashed into the drink holder in no-man's land in the van starts to smell like curdled milk.

So, if I feel the inspiration to write, I write. And try not to worry about dishes or toys. They will get cleaned up and dumped out and eaten on many more times before the day is over. I'm certain.

If my son needs a hug, I hug him. Even if I'm in the middle of cooking dinner and my hands are wet.

If my husband needs to tell me about his day, I stand there and listen. And try really really hard to keep my eyes on him and not on the toddler who is taking away his baby sister's toys for the thousandth time today. She will live. It will be okay.

Because like the Living Bible says in Ecclesiastes 11:4, if we wait for perfect conditions, we will never do anything. Why? Because perfect conditions don't exist. If we wait for our kids to stop fighting, our hands to not be wet, the dog to stop barking, or the kitchen to be clean, we will never get anything else done.

As busy moms and wives, shouldn't we know this?

Our lives exude less than perfect conditions, and yet, we try and try and try and think "If only" or "next time" or "when they are older." Not to be the bearer of bad news, but I'm not so sure things get that much easier when our kids get older.

A lady once told me after I had my second child that it doesn't really get easier as they get older, it just gets different. She's right. Some things may get easier, but other things get harder. New challenges, new stresses, new joys, and new lows.

What I am trying to say is this: Jesus calls us to do the things He calls us to do when He calls us to do them. Even—especially—in the middle of chaos. We have to do the important things God calls us to now.

Sometimes He calls us to sit still. Sometimes He calls us to be home. Sometimes He calls us to hang up our dish towel and hug our kids. To put down our phones and watch them play in the yard. Sometimes He calls us to speak to a group of women, join a Bible study, or start a prayer group. Sometimes He calls us to create, write, draw, paint, read, photograph, or sculpt.

Whatever He calls us to do, our job is to be obedient. To listen. To heed His instruction and not wait for perfect conditions. We will be blessed if we do. Maybe others will too. Again, not because we are great, but because He is and His plans are way better than ours.

It's easy to get bogged down by the chaos, but I don't want to. I want to remember the bigger picture—the kids that we are raising, the home we are creating, the words that are stuck in my gut and need to get out. I want to remember what is eternal and what is temporary and choose wisely. I want to be able to function in the chaos and I want the same for you. So does Jesus.

PRAYER

Heavenly Father, thank You for calling us to step out of our comfort zone and follow You. Whether it be loving an unlovable neighbor, writing a book, starting a business, taking a new job, going to a Bible study, or fostering a baby, we thank You that You've invited us on the journey with You, and we get to be blessed because of it. God help us to have courage where we lack it. We confess we are weak and prone to seek comfort, but Lord, You desire so much more for us. May we desire that, too. Help us remember what is most important in this life and fix the majority of our attention there, and let the cheeseburger sit in the back of van a little bit longer. (Okay, not too long, but give us peace while it sits there.) In Your holy and awesome name, we pray. Amen.

Moms and Muffins

"The virgin will conceive and give birth to a
son, and they will call him Immanuel" (which
means 'God with us'). Matthew 1:23

I had forgotten it was the "moms and muffins" morning at preschool. And so, I showed up to drop my son off in a wrinkled sweatshirt and jeans, no makeup, and a messy bun (not the cute kind). I'm fairly certain, I also forgot to brush my teeth, but some details are fuzzy. It had been one of those mornings, that detail is not fuzzy.

My superhero husband usually takes the kids to school, while I stay home in my pajamas with the twins and unload the dishwasher. But this morning he was out of town. And it was up to me to get five kids dressed, breakfasted, brushed, lunched, backpacked, and in the car by 7:15. Two schools, five kids, one van, and me.

Needless to say, my outfit was the least of my concerns. I

threw a sweatshirt over the T-shirt I slept in, pulled on some jeans and tied my hair back. That was about the extent of it.

I did roughly the same for my girls. I twisted a hair tie around the blonde rat's nest they wake up with so they looked a little less like they stuck their fingers in an electrical outlet.

But we made it. Barely. After nearly an hour of driving (God bless country life), we pulled into preschool at nine a.m. ready to drop and go.

Instead, we walked into a crowded room with tiered trays of muffins and galvanized metal basins filled with bottles of juice and coffee perched on ice.

Ahhhh, it was moms and muffins this morning. I forgot.

There were tablecloths and cute napkins, and little gift bags lined up neatly on a low table behind. Happy moms chatted with each other, the teacher, and their kids, looking so pleasant in their non-wrinkled clothes and mascara.

Then there was us, with our bedhead and rumpled clothes, straggling in. Now, I'm all about ponytails and yoga pants when you have no intention of doing yoga, so don't get the impression that I am usually dressed up when I drop my kids off at school. Slippers are my go-to when I know I don't have to exit the van.

But like…I hadn't brushed my teeth. I was basically wearing my pajamas to a party. Not a pajama one. And this was one of those sweet mother/son moments when he gives you a gift and you take a picture with him and his handmade trinket and post it on your Facebook page. It was one big photo op, and here I came in looking like orphan Annie. I wasn't so sure I wanted permanent documentation of how I looked that morning.

We stayed and we chatted because what other option did we have? We were already there. I drank juice and ate muffins and listened to the teacher read a story about moms. And when Lee handed me a white gift bag with a mug with a fingerprinted flower on it, I smiled and feigned surprise. I gave him a hug as he looked up at me wide-smiled, eyes sparkling, and dimples showing.

I watched as other moms got down on one knee to take a picture with their porcelain mug and beaming big-cheeked preschooler. And I knew what I had to do. How could I not?

How could I not show that I delighted in this little boy and his beautiful Mother's Day gift to me? How could I be so vain to care more about my appearance being immortalized forever, than him feeling the pride of posing for a simple sweet picture with his mom and his mug?

So although I was dying a little on the inside, I smiled and posed for the photo, like all the other moms. Because I realized, it wasn't about me or what I looked like, it was about being there with my son. He certainly wasn't concerned with my appearance that morning. All he cared about was that I was with him and he could give me the fingerprinted flower mug he made just for me.

That's all I should care about, too.

Because what if that's also all God cares about? What if He doesn't care what our hair looks like or whether or not we brushed our teeth? What if He is just generally glad we showed up to the party?

I think He is. In fact, I know He is.

The cool thing about showing up like I did that morning was that it was a chance to see Lee love me for me. And it gave others the chance to see the real me and say hi anyway. There was no facade, no pretense, no hiding the fact that I had completely forgotten about the party. But in the end, I was still at the party, and what I looked like didn't matter.

Jesus loves us for us. Because we are us. Not because we look nice, or act nice, or attend church on Wednesday night.

We don't have to look pretty for Him, because He already

thinks we are beautiful. We are His idea, after all, His magnificent, bold, intricate masterpiece.

I did post the picture on Instagram (you know I filtered it). I didn't have to. Lee would never know or care about that kind of thing. He doesn't even know Instagram exists. But that picture was proof I was there and it happened. And as I posted it, I remembered, I don't have to be perfect to be loved or to show up to a moms and muffins party.

So, as I go forward in my everyday life, loving the people God has placed in my world, I want to worry less about what I look like and think more about being present. Being present with God, fully known and fully loved, and present with my kids. Because being a mom, or a child of God, isn't about feeling pretty or perfect, it is about being loved right where we are, wrinkled sweatshirt, yoga pants, and all.

PRAYER

O Jesus, thank You that You love us—wrinkled clothes, smelly breath, and all. I will ever be grateful that I don't have to be perfect to be loved. I just am. We just are. Words cannot describe Your love, but it is ever-present and everlasting and independent of us. And You long for us to be where You are, which is why You paid the price for our sin, so we could make our home with You. May we walk in this truth today. Today, may we feel in our very souls the love we know in our minds that You have for us. May we walk in that truth today. Amen.

Tearing Down the House

"A wise woman builds her home, but a foolish woman tears it down with her own hands." Proverbs 14:1 NLT

I t had been "one of those days." I was halfway through a twelve-day stretch of solo-parenting, and I was pretty close to someone sticking a fork in me, because I was about done. My husband was ten time zones away in Africa, and I was by myself with five kids under seven.

While I was nursing one of my girls in the other room (as her sister lay crying on the floor), my three-year-old clogged the toilet with toilet paper. When I say clogged, I mean the overflowing-grab-every-towel-you-can-find-leaking-through-the-ceiling kind of clogged. I don't do clogged toilets. I wait for my husband to come home. But he was on the other side of the world and not coming back for days.

The twins had diaper rash and missed their afternoon nap. They were grumpy. I was grumpy. My boys had been fighting all day, whether it was wrestling, kicking, or pretending they were lions, it inevitably ended with someone crying.

All.

Day.

Long.

When bedtime finally came, I was so ready for them to be in their beds I could taste the chocolate I was going to stuff in my face once no little eyes were watching me.

Needless to say, I was less than patient getting them to bed. When they didn't listen immediately (as children do) I yelled at them. And when they still didn't listen, I yelled louder. I made heavy sighs and grunts and walked briskly about their room picking up clothes, huffing and puffing for them to brush their teeth.

It wasn't pretty. I was mean and I knew it, and I couldn't seem to help it. Have you ever been there?

I totally failed and I so badly wanted not to. I wanted to have some fun special time with them while their dad was gone. Maybe that was asking too much for one mom and five kids under seven. It most definitely was.

The next day my three boys were headed to their cousins' house for a few days. My sister-in-law graciously offered to keep them and give me some relief. I was grateful.

As I walked downstairs that night after the kids were in bed, exhausted and grumpy, mad at myself and honestly kind of mad at my kids, I saw their little camouflage duffle bags with their names embroidered in orange sitting neatly at the bottom of the stairs, and my heart broke a little.

My kids. My sweet little innocent kids. They were seven, six, and three, and here I was monstrously badgering them about picking up their clothes and brushing their teeth.

Sometimes I fail so miserably it hurts. It hurts my kids and it hurts me. I don't want my kids to remember me as angry all the time. I want them to remember me as fun, gracious, loving, kind, and understanding. And so often I am none of those. None.

Seeing those bags bursting at the seams with blankets and swim trunks, books, and stuffed animals, with their names emblazoned in orange, made me realize just how little they were, and it made me want to cry. I'm pretty sure I did, actually.

They are kids. My kids. And I love them like peanut butter loves jelly. They are literally part of me, and I'll always love them no matter how many times they ignore my commands to pick up their toys. But sadly, they wouldn't know it from how I acted tonight.

Proverbs 14:1 says, "A wise woman builds her home, but a foolish woman tears it down with her own hands."

Ouch. Ouchie. Tearing her house down with her own hands. That was me. I am the foolish woman!

You see, my family is my "home," and I am theirs. And when I yell at them, or get angry, or frustrated, or clench my teeth, I am tearing that apart. That stings.

I've done this with my husband before, too. There have been many times I have been jealous of the freedom he has. The freedom to dictate his own schedule, when mine is so closely tied to nursing and nap times.

But I've noticed, and perhaps you have too, that when I am jealous or angry or hurt, I don't respond in the best of ways. And instead of trying to build up my marriage, I start tearing it down with blame or envy. And it's so foolish.

I am hurt by the man I love, so I shut down, or blame him, or get upset. But that does nothing to deepen the bonds that I care about so deeply. In fact, it separates us even more! So the Bible calls it what it is: foolishness.

It's like that old saying, "if momma ain't happy, ain't nobody happy." As wives and mothers, we have a huge impact on the healthiness and happiness of our homes. If our emotions carry us away, others are likely to be carried away with it.

If you're like me, here's where you start whipping yourself like some Middle-Age monk. Please don't do that. Let's not beat ourselves up like that.

We are humans, prone to foolishness, in need of a Savior. That's it.

Motherhood is a beast of a job. A marvelous job, but a beast of one. Being a mother requires more patience than anyone can readily give. The demands are endless, and sometimes even impossible. We are gonna fail. We are gonna lose our cool. We are gonna yell. We are gonna hurt their feelings sometimes. It's a terrible truth, but it's the truth. We are human, and we need a Savior.

But just because we can be foolish at times, doesn't mean we are fools. If we claim to follow Christ, then He lives in us, and He has given us the power of life and godliness (2 Peter 1:3). So when I mess up, I pray. I ask God for guidance. I ask for His forgiveness, and I start over. I do the same with my kids and my husband.

Instead of being the foolish woman, I want to be the wise one. I want to build my house. I want to speak life into my kids and my husband. I want to give them a picture of grace, mercy, and unconditional love. I want to be their cheerleader, not their taskmaster.

I don't claim to know exactly what a woman can do to build her house instead of tear it down, but I do know it starts with the Lord. It starts by seeking Him with your whole heart. As we draw nearer to God, we become more like Him. And He. Is. Love. He knows how to discipline with love, purpose, and grace because He was the first Father, and He is a good one. And He also knows the ways between a man and a woman because He dreamed it up.

So I am going to keep on seeking God and His wisdom so I can be like the wise woman who builds her house, her people, and her world, instead of tearing it down.

PRAYER

Dear God, help us to be wise women instead of foolish ones. Help us build up those whom we love and not tear them down. Forgive us for the times we have done just that. Father, may we be filled today with Your love and with Your Spirit so that out of the overflow of our hearts, our mouths will speak peace and love. Lord, Your Word says how difficult it is to "tame the tongue" (James 3), but nothing is impossible for You! Keep doing Your good work in us, and as we trust You with the work You are doing in us, may it overflow into our households. With Your power and grace, may we build homes that are filled with peace, gentleness, patience, kindness, and self-control. In Jesus' name, amen.

The Angel in the Marble

"To them God chose to make known how great among the Gentiles are the riches of the glory of this mystery, which is Christ in you, the hope of glory." Colossians 1:27 ESV (emphasis mine)

My friend Amy shared a quote during a talk at our church, and it kind of blew my socks off. It is from the sixteenth century Renaissance artist Michelangelo. Of course. Who else could speak words like a knife to my mother heart? I know it sounds strange, but here are his words: "I saw the angel in the marble, and I carved until I set him free."

Is it just me or do you also feel the need for a moment of silence after reading this quote?

I don't know about you, but I feel the blade of the knife right now. God is shaving, carving, molding, and sanding me. It's nothing short of painful, and glorious, all at once.

Can you relate? Have you ever felt the cold edge of a chisel on your marble? Do you feel it right now? The sleepless nights and drowsy days. The crumbs on the table, car seat, rug—everywhere. The rotation of sleep, eat, and poop. The lonely days stuck in the house because little ones are sick—again. The spaghetti dinner that was thrown on the rug, the non-stop whining, and the continual strapping and unstrapping of tiny shoes, and the pulling of your hair as you bend down to help. The schlepping of kids and car seats, boosters, strollers and soccer balls.

Through the process of writing this book, with my hands very full, my kids have grown up. Alright, they are still here, they are still young, but we are suddenly out of diapers (even pull-ups) and almost training-wheel free. Now, we are battling fourth grade math homework, nighttime fears, an unknown job future, and the daunting task of teaching a kindergartner to read (again).

This season is new for us. Of course, each season we enter is new. And the carving I am going through now looks different than it did two years ago when I started this book. But it's carving nonetheless. Because God uses motherhood to mold us, shape us, and refine us.

It's hard being marble sometimes. (Pun intended).) But seriously, it is. While bits and pieces of yourself are being chipped away, it's easy to cry out in pain, "was that one necessary, God?" It's easy to second guess the artist. Does He really know what He is doing? What is His plan? Why is He doing this?

Maybe sometimes, when we feel the sharp edge of a sander or a chisel, we forget the purpose behind them. We think only about the pain we feel, instead of the vision the artist has for us. But here is the super cool thing about God, and the thing that brought tears to my eyes when I heard Michelangelo's words.

God sees the angel in us—and He longs to set it free.

He sees through our hard marble exterior, past our sin and imperfections, and sees something glorious deep inside. A new creation, a beautiful one. And His deepest desire is to set us free.

Free from shame, free from mom guilt, free from the worries that weigh us down and the sin that holds us back (Hebrews 12:1-2). He sees what you and I were made to be—in Christ. And so He carves—slowly, patiently, tenderly—so He can set it all free.

We are becoming new creations in Christ. The old being chipped away and the new being revealed (2 Corinthians 5:17). When it feels like the knife of God is pressing heavily against you, remember, the discomfort you are experiencing now is part of the process. The process of carving an angel.

When life is hard, I find comfort in this verse: "My son, do not despise the LORD's discipline or be weary of his reproof, for the Lord reproves him whom *he loves*, as a father *the son in whom he delights*." Proverbs 3:11-12 ESV (emphasis mine).

Those He loves. As the son or daughter in whom He delights! Not only does God do it because He loves us, but because He *delights* in us! The fact that God cares so very much about us is evidence that His discipline, His carving, is truly an act of His grace.

The chipping and sanding may be grating and unpleasant, but it is the only way to free the image underneath the stone.

Recently, I got the opportunity to visit England (a huge gift from God for this mom of five to cross the Atlantic) and we walked through the halls of Chatsworth. Owned by the Duke and Duchess of Devonshire, Chatsworth is one of the largest and wealthiest estates in Northern England. (It also happens to be portrayed as Mr. Darcy's house in the film *Pride and Prejudice*.) It is filled with thousands of works of art, from paintings, to furniture, draperies, tapestries, and sculptures. The sixth Duke, an enormous collector of art, filled an entire hall with marble sculptures.

As I walked along the corridor, standing in front of them, I was in awe of the detail. One woman the artist sculpted had ringlet curls surrounding her face. I wondered how long it would have taken to carve them. And how much patience.

So I did a little research and as I could have guessed, it can take years for sculptors to finish their figures. In fact, it took Michelangelo almost four years to complete his *David* sculpture. It is a process, friends, because it is an art form. It cannot be rushed.

And how much greater the undertaking, and possibly longer the process, for we who are much more than statues placed by a duke in a hall for all his rich friends to see. We are living eternal works of art on display for all people, to bring glory to God. I can think of no higher calling.

Trust Him. Trust the Artist. Trust the Master behind the sharp tool. He isn't just any artist—He is the first and finest Artist there ever was or will be. And in His infinite mercy He sees something in you and in me. Something, quite possibly, we do not. So be patient, our kind and gentle Sculptor carves and chisels and etches His vision on us so that something great will be revealed: Christ in us, the hope of glory. The glory that sets us free.

PRAYER

Heavenly Father, thank You so much for Your patience with us. Thank you for seeing Christ in us even when we don't. You see who we are becoming before we do. You see Your plans, Your purposes, and the character You want to develop in us, and so You grate and scrape and sand us into Your image. Thank You. It is a painful process, but we want what You want because it is always, always so much better. Please give us Your grace, patience, and peace to withstand the carving. May we fix our eyes on You and trust You as we begin to be set free. Thank You, Jesus, for this image and for the freedom You alone can give. Amen!

Two-dimensional life

*"And let us consider how we may spur one another on toward
love and good deeds, not giving up meeting together, as some
are in the habit of doing, but encouraging one another—and all
the more as you see the Day approaching." Hebrews 10:24–25*

I could have posted a picture of the Rice Krispy treats I made
that morning, and if you didn't know any better, you would
have thought it was a good day.

And if I had a few minutes more, the picture may have
actually been posted on Instagram, but I didn't and it wasn't.
Which may have not been a bad thing, because the crispy
treats are not what I will remember from that day.

I'll remember how I yelled. And I didn't take a picture of that.

I was making orthodontist appointments over the phone,
and my kids cannonballed (i.e. yelled, begged, screamed, kicked
each other) into the pool of my weak nerves, and when I hung
up the phone, I yelled so loudly I actually embarrassed myself.
So, I sent myself into time out. And while blow-drying my hair

and asking Jesus for forgiveness, I realized if you get a minute in time-out for every year old you are, I would need thirty-seven minutes to recover from this. Thirty-seven minutes sounded glorious. And impossible. With five kids under nine rambling around the house (two of them two), definitely impossible.

I took about ten. I got on my knees and prayed desperately for forgiveness and patience. I took some deep breaths. I blow-dried my hair.

I love my kids. And I'm old enough to know yelling is not what love looks like. Thankfully, we recovered. In the afternoon, I played air hockey with my oldest son and it was good. Then later that evening, he threw up. And that was that. That day was a mishmash of motherhood: good, bad, and ugly (in more ways than one).

But this devotion really isn't about yelling and patience, or kids and nerves, although I have a lot to say about that, too. It's about the parts of our lives we choose to share and the parts we forget to mention. It's about our need for genuine fellowship, because it challenges, encourages, and points us to what really matters.

You see, if I had ended up posting that picture of the sprinkled treats I made, my friends would have liked it and thought that I was having a good day. And I can't really say that I was, especially at the end of it.

I'm not saying that we shouldn't post pictures of the Rice Krispy treats we make for our children, or that we need to post about all of our parenting fails or illnesses. But I am saying that these pictures and posts never tell the whole story. Because they can't. Because they are two dimensional, not three.

Two-dimensional is defined as "having the dimensions of height and width only" (Dictionary.com). There is no depth in things that are two-dimensional. Isn't that like social media?

Most of what we do on our social platforms is catalog our

experiences, and generally, we want to remember the good ones, therefore those are the ones we post. That is perfectly normal and totally okay.

The problem is, it can get a little misleading. We can't fit the life and width and breadth of our entire day into a single post, we snapshot it. And we forget that even though pictures are worth a thousand words, there are still ten thousand more we could share.

It's easy to sit at home with sick kiddos, eating macaroni and cheese for dinner, scrolling through friend's posts of beach photos and Disney World, and think that your life is kind of blah.

But here's the reality: My life is no more blah than the next mom's, and hers no more exciting than mine. We both have our fair share of sick kids and yelling and macaroni and cheese. Maybe our clothes and our vacations are different, but the struggle is real for all of us.

And here's what else is real. You will never fully know what is going on in your friend's life unless you ask. Unless you give her a call, send her a text, or meet with her at a park. Only when we engage in the relationships in our lives are we given the honesty, perspective, and encouragement we so deeply desire and will never find online.

I love this passage in Hebrews, "let us consider how we may spur one another on toward love and good deeds, not giving up meeting together as some are in the habit of doing, but encouraging one another."

Give up meeting together? Never! But it happened during Paul's day and it is happening now. Sometimes our lives seem too busy for fellowship, but I'd argue that life is only meaningful in it. Fellowship with believers, with family, and with others in the same stage of life as us.

Social media is a weak substitute for this kind of fellowship. Yes, there can be support from online communities and social networks. Yes, we can be encouraged by a thought-provoking post or a word shared on Instagram. But true community is developed outside of it. Face to face. One on one. Life to life.

Real live friends add depth and warmth and meaning to the situations we find ourselves in, like the trickiness of mothering and the loneliness of homemaking.

"As iron sharpens iron, so one person sharpens another," says Proverbs 27:17.

One person, not one post. We sharpen one another when we share life with one another, the good, the bad, and the throw-up. (Alright, maybe hold the throw-up, but you know what I mean.) When we are vulnerable and real with our struggles, it encourages vulnerability and realness in others. And that's where the magic happens. Where we can "consider how we may spur one another on toward love and good deeds" (Hebrews 10:24), because that happens through relationship, through getting to know people not just on the macro level but the micro one. Knowing each other's struggles, doubts, fears, and temptations so that we can speak truth and breathe life into one another's souls. This is why we are to not give up meeting together.

As we sit and talk, laugh and cry together (even while chasing kids at the park), we can remind each other of the meaning there is in motherhood, the redemption that happens in it, and where we find the strength for it. In Christ.

No, the best way to encourage one another isn't through sharing our two-dimensional life, but our three-dimensional one. The one full of ups and downs, faults and forgiveness, trials and temptations, so we can see the full story of God's redemptive work in the lives of many. So let us not give up gathering, that we may build one another up and awaken each other toward what really matters—the redemptive story of God's love for us and the whole world.

PRAYER

God thank You for the relationships You have given us. Thank You for mom friends, thank You for non-mom friends, for older mothers, younger ones, brothers, sisters, parents and the list goes on. Thank You for creating relationships. Thank You for creating community. Relationships are not easy to find or to develop, so please help us here. Bring us into contact with people and friends who will speak truth, love deeply, and encourage us along this sometimes lonely journey. May we be those people to others as well. Give us the courage to share our struggles with one another, not seeking justification, but a chance to encourage and pray for one another. God, help us have listening ears and non-judgmental hearts. May we see You be glorified in and through these relationships You have given us.

Run, Walk, Crawl

"Not that I have already obtained all this, or have arrived at my goal, but I press on to take hold of that for which Christ Jesus took hold of me." Philippians 3:12

The thing about hills is, they stink. Let me explain. Last year we moved to a ranch in the golden hill country of California. It is beautiful—and, yes—hilly.

I am by no means a serious runner, but I try to run on a regular basis because it is good for my body and soul. Now that we live in "hill country," however, my runs have been much more challenging. Our driveway resembles the back of a camel. Even the shortest, fastest, easiest distance for me to run has one hill too many that I am forced to climb before I can head back home.

Hill country comes with all kinds of hills. Small ones, tall ones, short and steep ones, and my least favorite—the long slow gradual ones. These hills may not be steep, but the sheer distance they cover makes them the most horrific of all. It feels like I might possibly climb up forever. There is no break, no relief. Just a continual up.

Some days when I go out for a run, my legs feel like iron and I walk, because my mom-tired lungs and legs just can't do it. Some days, I feel great and I run like a champion (or the mom equivalent of a moderately successful runner).

When I am feeling great, my goal is to have a good pace. On days when I am feeling not-so-great, my goal is to simply run every single hill—no matter the pace. And on days when I am feeling even less than not-so-great (but running is still good for my soul), my goal is simply to get out there and do it—even if I have to walk the hills.

I used to get disappointed in myself when I had to walk, but I am starting to be less disappointed and more grateful that running shoes are on my feet and I am putting one in front of the other. Getting out there—even if I have to walk—is better than not getting out at all. Amen?

Motherhood often feels to me just like those hills. It is long slow work, and sometimes seems like a complete and total uphill battle. If it's not one thing, it's another. If it's not sleeping through the night, it's battling the nap. If not a fever, then it's lice. Or both. Or a work trip mixed with a last-minute science project.

Some days, I kill this mom gig, like I kill those hills. I've got my happy face on, a clean kitchen, a candle lit, and cookies waiting for them when they get home from school. Other days, the mom gig is killing me. Last night's dishes are still in the sink, candles are the last thing on my mind, and somewhere someone has colored on the wall.

But I am learning, like the apostle Paul, the secret of pressing on. Pressing on doesn't mean we feel like victors. In fact, maybe it can mean quite the opposite. We feel weak and fragile, and so, we press on.

Like being a mom, running isn't always easy or pretty for me, but I keep going, I keep showing up and tackling those hills. Why? Because it is good for my body and soul. Through the continual showing up, I'm realizing that walking does not mean I have given up. Walking may be a sign of a weak body, but it is not a sign of a weak spirit. And God is always more concerned with our spirit, than our body. For the spirit is willing, but the flesh is weak (Matthew 26:41).

So when I walk those long slow stinkin' hills, I am reminded that God isn't concerned with my pace, or the fact that I have to walk through tough seasons of life and motherhood instead of run joyfully. It does not matter to Him if I am huffing and puffing as I walk uphill or if I am running like Eric Liddell as I crest one. He just wants to see me out there. He just wants me to try, to show up, to put one foot in front of the other and be obedient to the call and work He has put before me.

The apostle Paul knew this. He was human just like me (though sometimes I wonder). But if there's one thing Paul seemed to master in his life here on earth, it was this idea of "pressing on" or continuing. The man had grit; he never gave up.

Paul knew he hadn't obtained perfection, obtained all that God desired him to be, but that didn't stop him from continuing. He kept going, seeking to take hold of that which God took hold of Him. Grabbing onto his Father (Philippians 3:12).

God is not concerned with our pace; He is concerned with our progress. And progress, slow as it may be, is still progress. Let the heavy load of perfection fall on Jesus, pick up your tiny cross, and press on to follow Him.

Press forward like Paul, dear busy, tired drowning friend. Press on through the poopy pull-ups when you are certain they should be going on the potty by now, through the sleepless nights when you think you are doing it all wrong. Through nursing, through sickness, through rushed school mornings, dirty vans, never-ending baseball games, and heaps and heaps of laundry (clean and dirty).

Sometimes you may run, sometimes you may walk, and sometimes you may crawl, but whatever you do, just get out there. Because God loves you when you are running; He loves you when you are walking; and He loves you when you're dragging.

Don't give up. He is rooting for you. So am I.

PRAYER

God, I thank You that Your love for us doesn't depend on our progress. You don't love us anymore when we run than You do when we crawl, and for that I will always be grateful. Thank You for rooting for us, for being our biggest fan, and never giving up on us. Help us this day, this day, as we go about it. Whether today is a day we feel at our best, or our worst, or some combination of both, may we find peace in knowing we are loved through it all, and You are just glad we showed up and didn't roll over and call it quits. Give us strength as we go today. In Your name we pray, amen.

The Other Thing About Hills

"No discipline seems pleasant at the time, but painful. Later on, however, it produces a harvest of righteousness and peace for those who have been trained by it." Hebrews 12:11

Last Thanksgiving, something miraculous happened. I got second place in my age group in the Gobble Wobble 5K.

Okay, yes it was the Gobble Wobble, and yes, it was second place, and yes, it was just my age group, so maybe that doesn't qualify as miraculous. But ladies, I do not consider myself to be a fast runner. In the ninth grade when I was playing soccer, possibly. But these days? These days are much different. The only sprinting I do is when I hear jumping in the bathtub or my son asks for glue.

But it's true. I ran three miles, each consecutively faster than I ever have, and I think I have the horrible hills at my house to thank. Turns out, hills make really good teaching material for God. And the second thing I am learning about hills is they make you stronger.

89

Hebrews 12:11, says that no discipline is pleasant at the time, but painful. I could not agree more. Running all the hills at my house is painful, not pleasant. They are hard. Really hard.

There's a quote about running my husband loves to say, "Running is like beating your head against a wall—it feels best when you stop." Word.

However, the running of hills has produced a speed and a strength in me I never had before. Those long slow inclines I detest have been building my muscles. They are giving me resilience and the ability to run faster than I thought possible.

That's the glory of doing hard things. The more we survive, the more we can survive. That's the glory of following Jesus; of going through trials and tribulations with Him, because the more we survive with Him, the more confident we are in Him and the more certain we are of His sovereignty.

I never imagined I would have five children. I always imagined four, max. And maybe it's a little ridiculous, but that one additional child really threw me off my game. (Not that I was always winning at it anyway.) But really, five? It seemed to catapult us into a whole new family category. It's like the difference between thirty-nine and forty. It's only a year—but it's a different decade.

Five kids make the minivan too tight. They make McDonald's expensive. We can't even fit at our own patio table without pulling up a kitchen chair. People just don't make things, cars, tables, or hotel rooms, with families of seven in mind. Cue the world's smallest violin playing for me. I know. I do love our big family, and I know twenty years from now when our Thanksgivings consist of twenty people (I'm already counting on a few grandkids) with just immediate family, it is going to be amazing. For now, it's mostly a lot of work and stretching and patience and things that don't always come naturally to me.

And so, if life is like a racecourse, the hardest hill for me to climb has been motherhood.

I am ever being stretched through it. Challenged by it. Disciplined in it. God is using motherhood to teach me that the hard parts build character. They push us, they shape us, and they teach us about endurance. Of course, I wouldn't trade any of it for anything, because although it is that hard, it is that good.

I think back to the days when my first son was born and how my heart seemed to grow ten times. Life was full of the beauty of new life, but also full of the unexpected. Like the C-section I had, and the newborn hearing screen he never passed. (He wears hearing aids now). Then fourteen months later, God gave us another son, and what had seemed difficult before now seemed impossible.

But it wasn't, because it continued. And then there was that time we lived in a hotel suite for six weeks with two kids under two and a dog and my husband worked a million hours. And then we moved across the country and started running a business. Then there were twins. And moving to a ranch.

And I think back to all those times I thought I couldn't do it—and yet I did. We did. Jesus and me (and my hubby too). In His everlasting strength, we prevailed.

Because God is so great, He loves us enough to discipline us and teach us how to overcome hardship, how to show up, and how to press on when the hills are much longer and harder than we ever anticipated.

The discipline of coming to the end of ourselves and relying on Jesus is painful. A lot like running hills—maybe a little like beating your head against a wall?

But it is training us. The discipline of doing hard things is cultivating a harvest of righteousness and peace in us. The righteousness not of ourselves, but of Jesus in us, and the peace that only He can give.

These troubles, these hills, these overwhelming things about being a mom are working for a greater glory that far outweighs them all (2 Corinthians 4:17). The eternal glory of Jesus revealed in us now and for all eternity. Thanks be to God!

PRAYER

Thank you, Jesus, that Your discipline produces righteousness in us. You are such a good God that even bad things become good things. What a gift. These trials we go through are achieving a glory in heaven that outweighs all the hard stuff we go through down here. Thank You. God help us to see these trials we go through as opportunities for growth and creating a glory for later, so that, as James says, we can "count it all joy" (James 1:2). Amen!

Walled in Junk

*"Come to me, all who labor and are heavy laden,
and I will give you rest." Matthew 11:28 (ESV)*

Down the street from our elementary school is a little old dilapidated farmhouse. Some windows have been boarded up and others are wide open, no longer windows but holes leading into a dark and drafty house. The paint is peeling, the roof, barely there. It has obviously seen much better days, a long time ago. But it is one of those houses I drive by and wish I could restore. To me, these old farmhouses are gems among the hills. They speak of a time gone by. I love their lines, their porches, and the character they hold.

However, not only is this cute little white farmhouse on the brink of collapse, it is surrounded by junk. Lots and lots of junk.

I have always noticed the junk. Floor to ceiling boxes are piled in rows and rows on the little wrap-around porch. So much so, that you cannot even see where one might enter this little farmhouse. There are cans of something, a couple lad-

93

ders, furniture, and who knows what else.

One day, as I was driving by this house once again, dropping off my boys for school, I noticed a man out front with what looked like a table saw and some bags of concrete. There were poles placed in the ground and concrete blocks being laid. It looked as though they were building a wall.

Sure enough, that is exactly what they were doing. A few months later, the cement wall was completed, painted, with a gate fastened in the middle. Even though the junk was not pretty to look at, somehow, the wall was actually worse. Instead of an old white farmhouse sitting on a hill in need of love and repair, there stands a cold cement wall, characterless and bland and completely impenetrable.

Obviously, I don't know the family or the reason they built the wall, but my guess is, they built it to hide what lies behind it. Maybe they were getting threats from the county or neighbors on the unsightliness of their junk. I'm not sure. But I do know, instead of cleaning up the junk, throwing away the outdated, the broken, and unusable things they built a wall around it. A wall to hide their junk.

I wonder sometimes if we don't do the same. Instead of dealing with the ugly and broken parts of ourselves, we build a wall around it. A wall so no one can see. A wall so no one can complain. Walls so that everything looks nice and neat on the outside, but all the while chaos waits within.

But here's the thing about walls. Walls hide. They protect. They keep trespassers out. They intimidate. They also isolate. Walls do not make friends.

When we build walls, we close ourselves off from the landscape and become our own little prisons where our brokenness can remain safe and alone and we can remain full of junk. To me, that beige cement wall isolates the farmhouse much more than the junk ever did.

Walls aren't built in a day. It took several weeks for that man to build a wall. I wonder if it would have taken the same amount of time to sort through the junk, save what was valuable, and toss the rest. I wonder.

We have the same choice.

We can spend time building a wall around our trash, or we can spend the time throwing it away. Separating the good from the bad, the memories from the meaningless, the useful from the useless. Instead of placing rebar in the ground, we should be tossing the stuff that weighs us down and burdens us, because it's hard to see the valuable things when there is so much junk in the way. We need to dump the junk.

Instead of helping us build walls, Jesus wants to help us sort through all the stuff. He wants to enter into our mess and help us decide, "worth keeping?" or "throwing away?" Most of it, we already know, is garbage. But He stands there, patient and kind, as He holds up a box filled with broken kitchen utensils and waits for us to realize their uselessness.

He says, "come to me, all you who are weary and burdened, and I will give you rest. Take my yoke upon you and learn from me, for I am gentle and humble in heart, and you will find rest for your souls. For my yoke is easy and my burden is light" Matthew 11:28-30.

We are burdened with junk, with selfishness and self-righteousness. With pride and envy and comparison. We are burdened with worry or anger about our circumstances. In short, we are burdened with sin. We are weary of running the motherhood rat race and trying to keep up with those proverbial Joneses. And as the rubble weighs us down, like the hoarders on the TV show, we start to feel buried alive.

But Jesus gives rest to our souls. He unearths the treasures hidden under the trash. He redeems, restores, and revives. He takes our burdens and gives us His rest in return. Peter advises us to cast "all your anxieties on him, because he cares for you" 1 Peter 5:7 (ESV).

Jesus comes in and gently cleans up the garbage, sorting the valuable from the harmful, casting out our burdens and our sin, and placing His much lighter and gentler burden on us instead.

When we invite Jesus into our heart to do this good work with us, we become a farmhouse worth saving, not hiding.

So can I ask you where are you building your walls? Where am I? Where are we keeping people out? Where are we keeping Jesus out? Are we hiding behind the wall of "I have it all together" or "my marriage is perfect" or "my kids have straight As and have memorized the Bible."

Walls have never made very good friends. As moms, if we know one thing, it is that we need Jesus and we need friends. We need compatriots with whom we struggle and strive and overcome the curveballs that motherhood inevitably throws.

So instead of building walls, let's invite Jesus in to help clean up the junk. And if the walls are already there, let's break them down. With Him at the forefront, we can wade through the mass of stuff, pick out the good, and chuck the rest. Let's rent a dumpster (or three) and purge. Let's restore what was broken. Un-board windows, replace the siding, paint the walls and salvage all the good we can. Because there is a lot worth saving—and a lot worth throwing away.

PRAYER

Dear Jesus, enter into our messy house today. Lay our hearts before You and help us sort through the junk that weighs us down and toss it out once and for all. May we confess our sins to You, and to those we have sinned against today and receive Your forgiveness and peace. Where there is sin we don't even see, point it out to our blind eyes. Tear down (ever gently, please, Lord?) the parts of our lives that need remodeling. It's a scary thing to pray, but we pray You bring the junk up from the basement so we can sort it out and get rid of it. Give us grace in this as well. If there are any walls we have built to hide behind, God break them down—again gently. I thank You that You are kind and humble and gentle as You work with us. And as we trade our burdens for Yours, we will find rest for our souls. Thank You! Amen!

Village People

*"Carry each other's burdens, and in this way
you fulfill the law of Christ." Galatians 6:2*

The first day she came to our house I wasn't so sure. We had never hired a nanny before. Sure, we've had lots of babysitters, but we've never had regular help, scheduled help we could rely on.

It wasn't that I was unsure of her, it was that I was unsure of the whole thing. I felt silly having someone come and help when I did not work outside the home. And here she was, a young twenty-something girl from church, whom I would have loved to impress with how I had it all together so that she would look up to me. But the very fact that we hired her meant that we didn't.

The first day she came in the back door. The one that comes through the laundry room. Horror of horrors. Instead of walking into the front door like most people, where things were relatively neat and organized, she parked where we parked and walked into the messiest room in the house. The room where I stuff anything

I don't know what to do with—plus all of our dirty clothes.

I remember I sheepishly asked her to use the front door next time. It was awkward. I probably embarrassed her. But I still had enough pride to be uncomfortable with people seeing the underbelly of our house.

At first it was hard and awkward watching her wash our dishes and fold my kids' pajamas while. I. Was. Home.

We flexed between employer and employee and friend and acquaintance. But the more we became sure of each other, the better it got. And I began to relish the fact that she cleaned up my kitchen and folded the laundry sitting in baskets next to the couch. The afternoons she came, gave me a breath of fresh air. It allowed me to help the kids with homework and not be overwhelmed with dirty bowls and spoons when it came time to make dinner.

The fact that she picked up my middle son from school two days a week, allowed me to not spend half the day in the van with my girls. (Country problems.) And when she was home, it gave me permission to leave the house, go for a run, or lock myself in a room to try to write this book.

Jessica has given our family breathing room. She has helped to carry the burden of raising five wonderful dependent children, while trying to write, run a business, and keep our marriage alive and well.

I knew finding help would give us that. But what I didn't expect was the relationship. The relationship she has found with my kids, and I have found with her.

Sometimes I find myself talking with her for twenty minutes in the kitchen before I head to the grocery store. And some nights, we come home from a date and hear her retell the bedtime conversations she had with our kids about heaven and hell and living for eternity. She has literally become an extension of our family and it is a beautiful thing.

One of the things I am learning in the process of living life with my hands overflowing is that not only is it okay to need help, it is part of God's plan for our lives.

"Carry each other's burdens, and in this way you fulfill the law of Christ," Galatians 6:2 says.

When we ask for help to carry our burdens physically or spiritually, we are building relationships with those around us and allowing them to love like Jesus loves.

Where we currently stand, Jessica carries our burdens way more than we carry hers. Still, if there is anything I give in return, it may be simply that I am another adult in her life who is cheering her on, seeking her best interest, and hopefully sharing some encouragement and truth along the way. Maybe someday I'll get to do more than that, but for now, it seems enough.

I think one of the reasons we are scared to ask for help is we don't want to look weak. We'd rather have the appearance of being strong. We want people to think well of us, to look at us and secretly say, "I want to be like her."

We are afraid the awful truth will get out that our house is really a mess and our kids are really wild. But the irony is, in order for our homes to be cleaner and our kids to be less wild, sometimes we need help.

There are seasons when our need for community, our need for help carrying our burdens, is stronger than others. And being a mom of little kids is definitely one of them. We won't be in this phase of life forever—although it sure feels like it. One day, our babies will sleep through the night, our children will poop on the potty, tie their own shoes, and stop rubbing Vaseline into the carpet.

But while the chaos reigns, let us boldly wave the white flag and surrender it to God. Let us let God help, and His people help too. Because I am becoming more and more convinced, our momentary humbling feelings of embarrassment or insufficiency will be quickly replaced with welcome feelings of refreshment and relief, for both parties involved. And that's a trade I am willing to make, even if it means having someone else fold our underwear.

And the amazing thing is, as we seek out the help we so desperately need, relationship happens. And as time goes on, instead of looking weak, we look human. We become relatable.

I think this has happened with Jessica. Turns out, I am mentoring her in a way after all.

Not with a perfect house or perfect children, but with the real and regular parts of our lives. She sees it all—well, most of it. And she seems to still love us anyway.

One of the blessings of following Jesus is belonging to the body of Christ, a group of people we can do life with. We were made for this, for relationship. We were made to rub off on others, as they rub off on us. We were made to carry each other's burdens and so fulfill the law of love that Christ has given us.

My encouragement to you, mom friend, is gather your village people. Find a friend, a family member, a neighbor, a babysitter who can help you in your hour (or hours) of need. It doesn't make you a failure to use village people to take care of your life, kids, work, and marriage. It just makes you a mom, and a part of a community some people call the village, we call the body of Christ.

PRAYER

Jesus thank You for all the Jessicas out there! Thank You for babysitters, nannies, neighbors, and friends who You give us in different seasons of life. Lord, bless them! And, Lord, help us find them! And when we find them, help us be humble enough to use them! Help us overcome the temptation to feel like we have to have it all together on our own. May we wave the white flag and ask for help. We weren't meant to do this life alone. In addition to Yourself, You have given us each other, a body, a community, a village, to surround us and help us live life. If we don't have community, please send us people to help in our hours of need. And one day, may we get the chance to be the body of Christ and help others bear their burdens. In Jesus' name we pray. Amen.

Peace and Powerlessness

"You keep him in perfect peace whose mind is stayed on you, because he trusts in you. Trust in the LORD forever, for the LORD GOD is an everlasting rock." Isaiah 26:3–4 ESV

W e just spent two and a half days without power. After two-years of horrendous record-breaking wildfire seasons in California, PG&E turned off our power as a precautionary measure because of predicted high winds and warm temps that could be dangerous in creating fires.

We received ominous notifications through text and a call to our landline the night before the power went out. "Due to weather forecast PG&E may turn off power on 10/09/19. Prepare a plan," it said.

A foreboding message to receive. Impending doom. No power. Prepare a plan. Our neighbor, being in the know, had graciously warned us of the probable power shut off days before PG&E sent their message. She told us to plan on going without power for three to five days.

Three to five days? Going without power for three to five hours on a stormy night is much different than three to five days of no lights or running water. We had to prepare. Prepare for the high winds and the zero electricity.

So we did. We flipped over the trampoline, took down the porch swing, put the bikes away, picked up the toys strewn around the yard, and closed up the barn. We filled our bathtub with water, we put batteries in all the flashlights, we found the camping lantern, and we hooked up our generator (which ended up being useless because it busted when we turned it on). We charged our phones and computers and made sure we had tons of paper plates and plastic silverware. I had all the children bathe. You guys, I even washed almost every single piece of laundry in our entire house—which is a feat in and of itself *and* I vacuumed all the rugs. (Somebody please give me a high five.) Serious mom points here. I need a sticker.

We went to bed that night a little anxious, but as ready as we could be. Then sometime around midnight, the fans stopped moving and the whole house woke up. Why oh why have we encouraged this addiction to white noise? None of us slept well that night. The girls wandered into our room crying for the fan to be turned back on. How could we explain to them we couldn't? They eventually fell asleep next to our bed on the floor.

Not having electricity is a really hard thing for three-year-olds to understand. Why won't our fan work at night? What happened to the night light? Why can't we watch cartoons?

The next morning, I sat sleepy-eyed in my robe, sipping my coffee (don't worry—we figured out a way to make that) as the sun lit up the room, trying to explain all these things to her.

My daughter's solution was we needed a new fan and a new TV.

I tried to explain that the problem wasn't with the TV or the fan. It was with the power source. We can try and turn the television on, but it won't work because there is no power.

"Why can't we turn on the power?" she asked, her barely visible eyebrows questioning me.

"I wish we could but we can't. We don't have the power to turn on the power," I sympathized.

It is out of our control. So we sit and we wait. We don't have power, and we don't have the power to do anything about it. We are powerless. In more ways than one.

The reality of this statement hit me hard.

We are currently in a season of waiting, and feeling a little powerless. We sit and pray and seek God for what the next steps will be, but ultimately, it is up to Him to move. We can't force our way out of this liminal space we are in. Liminal space. It's a new term I learned this year. Liminal space is the time between one thing ending and the next beginning. A wandering of sorts. Like the Israelites in the desert. Sounds delightful, doesn't it?

Whether or not you find yourself in an in-between place in life, the reality is we are all powerless. "Many are the plans in a person's heart, but it is the LORD's purpose that prevails," says Proverbs 19:21.

Jesus Himself said, "Apart from me, you can do nothing" (John 15:5).

No, we don't have control over the storms that come our way or the circumstances that surround us. But you know what we do have, don't you? We have access to the One who has the power. He has all the power in the universe and calms all the storms life can throw at us.

And still something more. While we didn't have the power to turn on the power for those few "Little House on the Prairie" days, we did have power over our attitudes on how we would weather the storm. We could choose to make the most of it, or we could choose to despair.

Having received a warning, we also had the power to "prepare a plan," as they suggested. We could have ignored the warnings, hoping it wouldn't actually happen. Or we could have prepared for the worst and hoped for the best.

We have the same choice in trials.

Like the ominous message from PG&E, Jesus warns us in the same way. "In this world you will have trouble," He says (John 16:33). Trouble is part of life. Suffering is real. Storms come in all heights, widths, and depths. Are we preparing our hearts for them? Are we getting to know and trust our Lord and Savior more each day?

I'm sure there is not a person out there who likes to think about brewing storms, or the various suffering we may experience in this world. Jesus knows this, because He knows us, and so the following words He says bring us comfort, reassurance and victory.

"In this world you will have trouble. *But* take heart, I have *overcome* the world" (John 16:33, emphasis mine).

We will have trouble, but we also have one so powerful He overcame the entire world and every trouble that is found in it! We don't have to be afraid. He is for us, not against us. He fights for us. He overcomes for us. He loves us.

Jesus also says in John 16:33, "I have told you these things, so that in me you will have peace."

He gives us warning to give us peace. Peace.

Peace was something we miraculously had those two and a half days without power. We knew the "suffering" was temporary. We knew PG&E was working hard to restore our power. We knew it would come back eventually. And that thought, along with the fact that we were prepared to go without it for days, gave us much peace as our egg cartons soaked in a cooler full of ice and the dirty dishes piled up.

So it is with us in all the trials in life. "You keep him in perfect peace whose mind is stayed on you, because he trusts in you" (Isaiah 26:3 ESV).

When we *know* the Jesus we fix our eyes on, the One who overcame, the One who gives peace that passes understanding (Philippians 4:7), and the One who is our rock (Psalm 94:22), we will be kept in "perfect peace" no matter the magnitude of the storm.

So when you feel helpless and powerless, remember Who isn't. And whether you are going through a storm right now or not, it is helpful to remember that storms are a part of the human experience, and also—they won't last forever. While we don't know what future trials may be, the best way to prepare for them is by getting to know the One who is bigger and stronger than anything else that could come our way. And once the storm comes, we simply cling to Him because we trust Him—and we will be kept in perfect peace.

PRAYER

Heavenly Father, You are so powerful! You are holy! We can't begin to comprehend Your mind and plans and purposes. We are just itty-bitty little beings who need so much help. But we have access to the Creator of the universe, so how can we truly lack anything? Oh Father, may we long to know You deeper. May we be drawn closer and closer to Your heart, so that when trials come, we can know the One in whom we trust and be kept in perfect peace. I thank you that when we are powerless, You are not, so when we have You, we have everything we need. Amen!

The Puppy Dog Tree

"For just as the heavens are higher than the earth, so my ways are higher than your ways and my thoughts higher than your thoughts." Isaiah 55:9 NLT

We were driving to a baseball game and my seven-year old was sitting shotgun. It is a position he does not usually get, mostly because I think it's against the law in California. But it was one of those times we had to put the third row seats down to jam the trash can in the back of the van because Dad was out of town and the truck was in the shop. (In the country you have to do some crazy things like *drive* your trash cans a mile down the road so they will pick them up.) Thus, the rest of the car was filled with kids and car seats and the only open spot was up front.

It was a whole new experience for both of us having him ride next to me. I found myself explaining what "PRDNL" means and how to work (and not work) the temperature controls. Everything was new and exciting to him. It was a joy watching his enamored face as his eyes scanned the bounty of all the front passenger seat had to offer. But the best thing he gave me on that fifteen-minute drive to the ball field was a new perspective.

"Mom, I want you to see this tree. It looks like a dog." Hmmm, a tree that looks like a dog. I wondered if I would see it, too.

We missed it that time as we sped past onto the baseball game, probably running late. But the next time we were in the van as we drove down the same road, he yelled from the back row, "Look mom! There's the tree; doesn't it look like a dog?"

Then I saw it, and it did. It looked exactly like a dog. I had driven by this tree a thousand times before on the way to school, to baseball, to the park, to church, the grocery store, and to hang out with friends, but never had I noticed how much this tree looked like a dog, exactly like a dog, floppy tail and all.

That is the gift children give us. The chance to see things we never saw before. The chance to see things from a new point of view. Perhaps that is why Jesus loves them so much. They aren't too busy or too jaded to see. Their ears are open, so are their hearts, and they live free.

The week before, I had spoken to about 100 women at a ministry at our church. I spoke about beauty, a topic that is near and dear to my heart. Afterwards, I felt like it didn't go so well. I wondered if my heart really came across. I replayed in my head things I said and how I wished I had said them differently. I lost my place several times in my notes and felt generally off about the whole thing. It was so bad I thought maybe I should never speak again.

I called my mentor and friend, the head of women's ministry at our church, and shared my heart. I asked her to be honest with me about how my talk went. She was encouraging and truth telling. Then she called me a few days later and told me a story.

A mother and daughter had wanted to come to our Saturday morning get together but had forgotten to register. They came an hour late, when they knew the food would already be eaten, and the speaker would be speaking. They came and they sat outside the doors to the chapel just so they could listen.

Afterwards, the two of them went to lunch and the daughter opened up. She told her mother things about her own struggles with being beautiful, the impossible standards and the mean things boys say. Things her mother never knew because they never talked about it. The mother e-mailed our women's ministry director the following day and thanked her for the transparency and conversation that was sparked between them because of our ministry.

God had plans that Saturday morning I knew nothing of. That shouldn't surprise me, but it did. What seemed like a failure on my end, was not on God's end. Even though I stumbled my way through my notes, forgot my place, and maybe said things that didn't come across very clear, God still used it.

All the time I spent rehearsing my mistakes was useless. I was inward focused. He was outward. He didn't care that I slipped up a few times. It was not about me or my job. It's about Him and His work. Far bigger, far greater reaching than mine.

It is crazy to me to think that God has plans for me, each one of my five children, my husband, my ministry leader, and the woman and her daughter who sat outside the doors. He has plans for my sisters and my brother, the teachers of my children, the principal at their school, and the people we pass on the highway. He has plans for the whole world. Every. Single. Person. And He weaves us all together in the most intricate and beautiful and unimaginable ways possible. It is too much to take in. That is why He is God, and we are not.

He is so immensely inconceivably vast that while we see one thing, He sees a million. We see one answer, one problem, one solution; He sees a hundred thousand times a hundred thousand. Maybe sometimes that looks like us seeing another plain tree, and Him seeing a puppy dog.

So it shouldn't come as a surprise that what I thought was a failure, God used for some good in other people's lives. He does this kind of thing all the time.

It encourages me as a mom. Who knows what God is doing with the seemingly trivial and infinitesimal things we do as mothers. They may not seem significant or life changing. They may even seem like failures, yet they have a purpose beyond what we can conceive. It's truly mind-blowing.

Now I cannot drive by this tree without seeing a dog. In fact, it has become the puppy dog tree to our entire family and a landmark to my kids that we are almost home. And each time, I am reminded that things don't always seem like they appear at first glance, especially in the Kingdom of God.

PRAYER

Father in heaven, You are holy. Your thoughts are not our thoughts, nor Your ways our ways. Yours are so much higher and so much greater, and for that we give You much thanks. Forgive us when we doubt and question You. What do we know? Who are we? We are Your humble servants, that is our desire. So, please, use our failures, our weakness, our humanity, and make something beautiful out of it. Because that is what You do and who You are. I thank You that while we see trees, You see puppy dogs. You are so good like that. And, Lord, how we pray that You would give us eyes to see puppy dogs, too. We want Your vision, Lord. In Your name we pray. Amen.

Terrible Gifts

*"'I tell you the truth,' Jesus said, 'this poor widow has
given more than all the rest of them. For they have
given a tiny part of their surplus, but she, poor as she is,
has given everything she has.'" Luke 21:3–4 (NLT)*

I t was Thursday afternoon and we were making our long
journey back from preschool to our house in the boonies.
Lee was sitting in the middle of the middle row, in between his
two little sisters and their expansive car seats, looking big and
small, all at the same time. I asked him what his favorite part
of the day was.

"Oh, I can't tell you that."

"Really?" I wondered, almost concerned, until his little ha-
zel eyes lit up and he smiled. "It's a secret. It's for you."

A half-second delay and then I remembered Mother's Day
was just around the corner.

"I'm making something for you," he beamed. "I hope you
like it."

"Of course, I'll like it," I replied.

"But what if it's terrible?" he asked, genuinely worried.

"You know I will always love anything you make me, Lee, because you made it." I smiled in the rearview mirror at him. He smiled a big one back.

As I said the words, it was like a truth revealed that I had always known.

I can't think of a mom who opens a Mother's Day card from her five-year-old and says, "You know, my hair is not pink or spikey. Oh, and you missed the nose, ears, and fingers. And how come I only have one leg?"

No, no, and no. What do we do instead? We ooooohhh and we ahhhhh and we hang them on refrigerators or clip them to chicken wire boards from Hobby Lobby. We display them on windowsills and desks and keep them in piles of paper we can't bear to throw away but aren't sure what to do with. We take pictures of them and save them somewhere in the cloud (wherever that is) or keep the originals in memory boxes. If you're amazing, you scrapbook them. Whatever we do with these pieces of paper, we savor them, because our children made them.

Admittedly, some of the artwork is genuinely adorable and funny, even beautiful in its own way. But at the end of the eighteen and some odd years, we hang on to these pieces of construction paper not for their beauty, or accuracy, the essence of life they captured, or their artistic impressions, but because our children made them—and gave them to us. And when they make things for us, what it looks like is beside the point.

What if my heavenly Father sees me just how I see my son? What if He loves every single thing I give Him, not because of what it is, or how good it is, but because I am the one giving it?

Sometimes I feel like I don't have a lot to give, and what I do have isn't good enough. At times, I feel this way about writing, raising kids, being married, having friends, and folding laundry. So little time, so little talent. People do it better than me.

Like Lee, I worry, too, what if I'm doing a terrible job? What if it isn't as good as someone else's? What if my laundry piles are bigger, my kids wilder? What if my words are too stale or cliché? My "ministry" too unorganized?

Will you still like it, God? Does it look okay? Is it enough?

But I am learning with God, it's never about the gift, always the giver. He doesn't care if we give Him two pennies or two thousand, as long as it is from our heart to His. That is all that matters to Him.

On this blessed journey I am learning that one of the best things about following God is you don't have to have a lot to give. You just have to give what you have. It is His pleasure to take care of the rest.

And what we give doesn't have to be perfect, or complete, or even enough, for Him to love it.

Sometimes, I forget. Like the poor widow at church, our offering can seem like a terrible gift. But Jesus knows it isn't, because He knows it is her all.

"But she, poor as she is, has given everything she has" (Luke 21:4 NLT).

When we write because He calls us to, when we love our kids like He loves them, when we fold laundry as an offering to Him, and put our small coins in the offering plate, He smiles at us from the driver's seat, because you see, He loves us. And love doesn't see a multitude of imperfections, but the heart behind it.

Our brush strokes don't have to be perfect. Our proportions can be lopsided and our renderings off base. Our time short, our words few, our creations so-so, our money little. We can draw people with one leg and no hands and God says, "I love it!!" And He really does. He is so gracious with us.

And so I hear Him say as He looks in the rear-view mirror at me, the little blonde five-year-old girl between two carseats and says, "You know, I will love anything you make for me, Brooke, anything you give to me, because you made it for me."

God loves us so incredibly much. Let us not be afraid of giving God "terrible" gifts, because if our heart is in it, to Him, there is no such thing.

PRAYER

Heavenly Father, thank You for receiving our gifts, whether big or small, beautiful or just so-so, and receiving them with enthusiasm because of Your great love for us. What can we say in response to Your great love? What gift can we bring? Only us. Our broken hearts, our wandering minds, and our weak bodies. But these are not terrible gifts, because we are valuable beyond measure to You! Thank You! O God, help us see ourselves as You see us, children worthy of our Father's love. And may we spread this kind of love to our children, our spouses, and those we come in contact with. In Your name, we pray. Amen.

Bad Bananas

"So I advise you to buy gold from me—gold that has been purified by fire. Then you will be rich." Revelation 3:18 NLT

So there was this man, this sweet little man wearing a red turban and a big smile, who sold me rotten bananas. True story. Let me explain.

A while back we decided to rent a cabin in a small town tucked away in the Sierra Nevada Mountains of California. It is a quaint town, full of little red buildings left behind by the mining company who once owned it. We arrived early, ready to settle into our cozy little cabin. But first we needed groceries.

The town had six hundred and some odd people, and the only thing resembling a grocery store was the famous General Store on Main Street. We are no fools. General stores sell trail mix and beef jerky. We would need more than that to feed our herd.

We headed to a slightly larger town down the road where we assumed we would find a real grocery store.

To our dismay, when we "Yelped" grocery stores, as every

good millennial does when arriving in a new place for the weekend, we only saw three names of places and none of them were Safeway—or even names we recognized.

We chose the red teardrop nearest our little blinking blue dot on the map. It didn't look like much from the outside, but I still had hope.

How could this town not have a grocery store? I wondered. Where did these people get their food? Here? I guess?

I walked into the little shop and almost immediately walked back out. As I glanced around, it seemed a little more than a 7-11, a few boxed goods with high prices.

Seeing me walk in and turn around, the man behind the counter quickly asked what he could help me with.

"Oh—well…" I said, "I am looking for groceries," and turned to go.

"Oh, but I have some here," he said in his very helpful voice.

"I mean, like produce—like bananas," I replied.

"I have some bananas," he said, and he walked me over to what looked like a deli shelf with two speckled bananas hanging from a hook. We are a family of seven. We need a literal bunch of bananas, not just two. "Hmm." I said, trying not to look too snobby. The bananas did not look good. But what were my options? Drive around to two other stores that didn't sound much more promising? We needed to get groceries and get to the cabin, before all the kids started to go bananas.

Well, I began to reason to myself, it's not exactly what I was looking for. None of it was. But it was close enough, I thought. And here he was so nice and kind, leading me all around the store to the items I asked for. They weren't quite right, but they weren't quite wrong either.

However, once we settled in at the cabin, we soon learned it wasn't just the bananas that were bad. The cheddar cheese tasted horrible and was covered in a thin white mold and the frozen peas were one solid chunk of ice. Nearly everything we opened from the store was bad.

Later that weekend my husband drove back up to town for something and saw a small-town supermarket called Leonard's. We also later realized the quaint old General Store actually did sell fresh produce, fresh meats, and other dry goods.

This nice and extremely helpful man didn't tell me that there was a grocery store a few blocks away. Instead, he took advantage of my ignorance, escorted me around his store helping load my arms with canned tomato sauce, a pint of eggnog, and a few ripe bananas, all the while there was a bigger store down the road. One that had a hundred fresh bananas and half an aisle dedicated to bread.

I felt like I had been taken and I was mad! But it wasn't all his fault—it was mine too. As we made do for the weekend with our expired food, I began to think how similarly I can act in other areas of life.

Instead of searching for more, I settle for less. Instead of desiring for God's best for me, I desire my best for me. I get comfortable in my comfort, and worse yet, comfortable in my sin. I think things like "this is as good as it gets," or "don't dream too big, it'll probably never happen." And so I go about life shopping in a convenience store, looking for joy and fulfillment in all the wrong places, instead of turning to Him.

It reminds me of this quote from C.S. Lewis:

"It would seem that our Lord finds our desires not too strong, but too weak. We are half-hearted creatures, fooling about with drink and sex and ambition when infinite joy is offered us, like an ignorant child who wants to go on making mud pies in a slum because he cannot imagine what is meant by the offer of a holiday at the sea. We are far too easily pleased."

Yes. Far too easily pleased. Far too easily acquiesced. We may question if this is all there is, but almost as soon as we have asked, we begin to accept the answer the world offers: yes. Don't dare dream of anything more. This is it. Be satisfied with your four-bedroom house, your comfortable church, and a trip to Disneyland.

I am not saying God wants us to have a bigger house, better friend group, or a different vacation. God's holiday at sea is not about a house, a car, or a job. It isn't about things at all. It is the joy that comes from being swept up into His story for His glory.

In our struggle to see God's vision, we would be wise to remember we have an enemy who desperately wants to keep us distracted with mud pies, instead of enraptured by the idea of a trip to the ocean.

Like the man with the big smile, our enemy wants us to buy things from his store. (Okay, I am not saying the man was Satan, but you know what I mean.) He doesn't want us to leave. He leads us around, showing us other options. Showing what he has to offer. We can see the problem. It isn't really what we wanted, but it seems close enough. And we believe the lie. We buy the bad food. We eat the moldy cheese.

The goods our enemy tries to fill our arms with never satisfy completely, because they weren't meant to. Marriage is great, but it doesn't bring fulfillment. Neither does motherhood, or work, success, or living the American dream. We look for satisfaction in these things, but God has a much bigger dream for us than the American one.

Like the Westminster Catechism states, His desire for us is that we would "glorify God and enjoy Him forever."

Friends, let's not miss it. Let us not miss God's dream. Let us not settle for the lies our enemy would have us believe. May we walk out of his corner market and into the bounty of a good Father. May we continue to believe that God has good plans for us, like He says in Jeremiah 29:11.

May we also believe that God, "is able to do *immeasurably more* than all we ask or imagine, according to his power that is at worth within us" (Ephesians 3:20 emphasis mine).

Like Jesus advises in Revelation 3, let us buy gold from our Father in heaven, and then we will be rich with what really matters. Rich in love. Rich in godliness. Rich in purpose. Rich in Christ. Off on a holiday at sea, instead of making mud pies on the street.

God open our eyes to see that there is a whole storehouse of food available to us, not just a few canned goods and some barely breathing bananas.

PRAYER

Dear God, forgive us. Forgive us for settling for less. Forgive us for believing the lie and getting suckered into things that look and feel okay, but deep down we know are not what we were after. We do not want the counterfeit junk. We want the real thing. We want true joy, peace, love, and satisfaction, and the only place we will ever find that in this world (and the next) is in You. Lead us to the fountain that never runs dry and to the store that has more than everything we ever dreamed of (Ephesians 3). You have infinitely more to offer than this world. You are such a good and loving Father. In Your name, we pray. Amen.

Constancy Over Consistency

"Jesus Christ is the same yesterday, today, and forever." Hebrews 13:8 NLT

I first heard about the idea of constancy over consistency through a marriage training I attended with my husband in the beautiful green mountains of northern Georgia at a little place called WinShape Marriage.

My husband and I were being trained as a "host couple" for marriage adventures, which sound glorious and some day we will do. Someday. As part of our training, they shared six key principles of a great marriage. One of them was *constancy*.

Constancy, the idea that our marriages might not always be consistent—some seasons will be great, and others less so, but our marriages will continue because we are committed to one another through thick times and thin ones. The simple comfort of knowing that we are a constant in each other's life.

The idea of constancy is not a new one, but thinking of it in terms of marriage, was. Of course, this makes a lot of sense. There have been seasons in our marriage that are effortless and other seasons that have been hard and required work. But through it all, we remain. We remain committed to one another, through the ups and downs, and that is what makes marriage great.

When it comes to parenting, there is a good amount of discussion about being consistent but hardly any about being constant. There are many books that stress the importance of consistent nap times and bedtimes. Consistent discipline, chore charts, and behavior. Consistent consequences and rewards.

I know all these things are good, and I have been a bit of a sleep Nazi myself with babies. I know consistency is important—especially for young children. But sometimes, consistency feels impossible.

Why? Because life throws us curves every single day. Because the sun rises and the sun sets, but on a given day with kids that is about all you can count on.

Family life is so very often not consistent.

And so, I continually worry that I am not doing all the right things for my kids. Consistency is hard. Throw in some PMS, toddler twins getting out of their cribs, and some baseball practice and it is even harder. Consistency goes out the window really fast.

But constancy is something different. Something altogether grander and somehow easier to achieve, because it has less to do with regularity, and more to do with faithfulness. It has less to do with getting it right, and more to do with being committed.

I can do that.

I may not always say and do the right things, but I am committed to my children. Committed to their growth and development. Committed to telling them about the goodness of God and the love and grace found in Jesus.

Sometimes, I may let one child off the hook easier than the other. I may let my daughter poop in pull-up one day and make her sit on the potty the next, depending on how I am feeling that day. But I am committed to my kids. I want them to grow into loved and confident young adults—and eventually poop in a toilet.

So every morning, I show up, bleary-eyed and blurry-brained as I may be, stumbling toward the coffee pot, because I am bound to see my kids get breakfast, pack a lunch, and get out the door to school on time. I am there because that's what a mom does. I brush their hair, wipe their bottoms, and tie their shoes because I love them and I am devoted to them.

I don't think there is enough said about the goodness of simply being committed. Of simply being there. Of the comfort of our presence, and the support our children feel when they *know* that no matter what, we will be there the next day. And the day after that, as long as God gives us breath, because we love them.

And when I think about God and all of His character traits, it is His unchanging nature, His constancy, that comforts me most.

Because if God is love, and that love doesn't change, then that means He loves me even when I feel unlovable. He is my Father in heaven and I am His child, and He is committed to me. I am His forever. And so, like His word says, He will never leave me or forsake me (Joshua 1:5).

The best part of His good, good character is that it never changes. Like Hebrews 13:8 says, "Jesus Christ is the same yesterday, today, and forever."

But something else I have noticed (and maybe you, too) is even though His character is constant, He doesn't always seem consistent. (This doesn't mean that He isn't, it just means we don't see it that way with our finite, ephemeral brains.)

Because sometimes people die from cancer before their thirtieth birthday. Sometimes parents die long before we think they should. Sometimes husbands leave their wives. Sometimes children get leukemia. And we don't understand. It doesn't seem consistent with a God who says He loves us.

But the truth is, cancer and divorce don't change the character of God. He is still the God He was the day the bad news came, as He is right now when the sun is shining, as He will be in the unknown of tomorrow.

And if His character is only good, and His character never changes, then we can find hope in the midst of heartbreak, comfort in the middle of pain, and joy as we look to the future.

When I was looking up the definition of *constant*, I was reminded of how it is used in mathematics. To refresh your ninth-grade algebra memory, a constant is "a number that is fixed and known, unlike a variable which changes with context" (vocabulary.com).

There are so many variables in our lives that change with context. From little things like sleep, mood, Daylight Saving, and newborn babies, to bigger ones like terminal illnesses, job loss, death, and divorce.

But there's one fixed thing, or should I say Person, in life who doesn't change with context. There is One who is constant. Our Father in heaven. And if I had to choose one constant in life to have, I couldn't think of a better one.

He is the fixed point I want to center my life around. In the middle of the rushing, the chaos and the changing nature of life with little ones, let us focus on the one true constant in life: our Father in heaven. Let us remember who is committed to us, who is faithful to us, "the one who is, who always was, and who is still to come" (Revelation 1:4 NLT). And then we will find peace and rest for our souls.

PRAYER

Father in heaven, thank You for being the One constant we can center our life around. When life throws us curveballs and when seasons change, You remain the same. Help us rest in this truth today. The truth that Your love never fades, and Your character "does not change like shifting shadows" (James 1:17). I thank You that we can count on You in this unstable, unpredictable world. May we cling to You today. Amen.

Hot Coffee?

"Draw near to God, and He will draw
near to you." James 4:8 NKJV

I f you're a mom like me, with your hands overflowing, you know the struggle is real when it comes to coffee. Gotta have it. Can't find time to drink it.

The mornings I wake before my kids are amazing. I can sit in silence in my bathrobe, sipping steaming coffee, reading my Bible, and journaling. Even if it's fifteen minutes, it's glorious.

However, the second those little darlings' heads pop off their pillows, it's making toast, getting water, packing lunches, signing papers, gathering homework, and the coffee gets put on the counter and forgotten. Sitting there in that cute ceramic mug with the scripted verse on the side, it doesn't take long for it to grow cold.

Cold is okay. I can drink cold coffee. I put so much cream and sugar in mine, it's kind of like an iced latte. Sometimes, I even stick it in the fridge so I can drink it later, on ice.

But what happens more often than not is I end up drinking lukewarm coffee. Countertop coffee. In attempt to recapture the glory, I stick it in the microwave for thirty seconds—and you guessed it—forget about it. By the time I remember, it's already had time to cool down. So, I try again. Take 2. Take 3. Eventually, it's just not worth the steps, and I live with it, guzzling the lukewarm coffee like the lifeblood it is.

But that's not how it's supposed to be. There's nothing savory about it, no joy in drinking not-so-hot coffee.

The other day, however, after *all* of my children had gone to school (thank You, God, for preschool) I wasn't satisfied with my tepid coffee so I reheated it, and with no kids around to distract me, I remembered it. I reached my hand through the white door and out came piping hot coffee with little swirls of steam rolling off the rim of my mug, and I smiled.

Ahhh, yes. Hot coffee. This is how coffee is supposed to be. Like the first cup I get on those dark quiet mornings when I am awake before my kids. Coffee is meant to be enjoyed steamy hot (or icy cold), but definitely not room temp.

When I think of this coffee problem, I can't help but be reminded of that infamous Bible verse about God wishing we were either hot or cold.

"I know all the things you do, that you are neither hot nor cold. I wish that you were one or the other! But since you are like lukewarm water, neither hot nor cold, I will spit you out of my mouth!" (Revelation 3:15-16 NLT).

Yikes! Apparently, God has a thing about hot and cold, too.

If growing cold means we are far from God and lukewarm gets us spit out of His mouth, then there is really only one option for the Christ-follower in this passage. We've gotta be hot.

What's even scarier for me is that if I'm being honest, a lot of my days are spent in the lukewarm category.

Living in America has its perks, but it also has its drawbacks. In a culture that is so very wealthy and so very independent, it is easy to feel like we don't really need Jesus. We are not wondering where our next meal will come from or walking miles for our daily water. We have all that we need, and abundantly more, literally at our fingertips.

But what we sometimes forget is that we are no different than any other human being on the planet. Completely dependent on Jesus and on our heavenly Father, to send the rains, to grow the crops, and to keep the power on. Without Him, we are nothing.

"For you say, I am rich, I have prospered, and I need nothing, not realizing that you are wretched, pitiable, poor, blind and naked. I counsel you to buy from me gold refined by fire, so that you may be rich" (Revelation 3:17–18 ESV).

When I feel myself growing cold, distant, or ambivalent to Kingdom things, I know something is wrong and something needs to be done. But oftentimes, I'm at a loss for what. I can feel distant even when I read my Bible. Have you ever felt that way? In the discipline, I can feel dry. What is the remedy for this?

Buy gold refined by fire from Jesus. Put on His garments and His salve on our eyes so that we can see clearly (Rev. 3:18). I think this means, meet with Jesus. Really meet with Him. Because He is there; He is waiting. He is standing at the door and knocking (Rev. 3:20) and wanting to come in and meet with us, to give us His true wealth to cover our nakedness and uncover our eyes so that we may truly see.

I certainly don't have all the answers, but I'm finding that if there's such a thing as a microwave reheat in my life, it's this:

Pour out my heart to Him.

Tell Him all the things I don't want to, but He already knows anyway. Tell Him how I feel distant, afraid, lonely, sad, or even angry. Confess my sins to Him and receive His forgiveness. Because again, He already knows all of my sin—and has decided to love me anyway. With a love that I can't un-do.

Sometimes pouring my heart out takes more than thirty seconds. Sometimes it takes thirty minutes, sometimes days, or weeks, maybe months, until I get to the things stuck deep down in my heart, but I keep pressing in because it's worth it.

And at some point along the way, as I press my soul against Jesus', I start to heat up. His warmth becomes mine, and my heart becomes tender again. My ears start to hear truth, real truth, instead of the things that have the appearance of it.

James 4:8 says that as we draw near to God, He will draw near to us. I've claimed this truth over and over in my life when I have felt distant from God—even in the midst of serving Him. Draw near. Just pull up a chair and talk. Pour. Give. And listen for His response.

I guess, in a way, it's like having coffee with God, in the truest sense of the words. (Hopefully hot coffee or iced if you prefer.) Because it also says in that same passage that He stands at the door and knocks. He is there, always has been, but He waits for us to open the door.

Open the door and begin a real honest conversation with Jesus. And if it's a little one-sided this time, that's totally okay. Perhaps it needs to be that way at first. After all, when you pour out your heart to someone, it usually is.

But don't stop there. Wait and listen. For He will respond. In His time and His way. Through His Word.

So, dear friend, if you're tired of feeling like a lukewarm cup of coffee sitting on the counter and are in need of a heat up like I often am, pour out your heart and tell Him everything. Open the door and draw near to Jesus—and He will draw near to you.

PRAYER

Holy Father in heaven, we confess we have sometimes been lukewarm. We feel we have all we need yet haven't realized that without You we are blind and naked and poor. I thank You that Your word says if we draw near to You, You will draw near to us. So, Lord, today we pour our hearts out to You. We draw near. We sit and we wait for You to fill us up and reheat our very souls. We want to be hot. Not cold. Not lukewarm. We want to be on fire for you. Make it so! In Jesus' name, we pray. Amen.

Moving Dirt

"Let us not become weary in doing good, for at the proper time we will reap a harvest if we do not give up." Galatians 6:9

A few months ago, we tore the back porch off our house. Literally. It was full of dry rot, so we demolished it and replaced it with a cement patio. I say we, but really, it was my husband. I think I held the ladder once, at least. Maybe one day, we will put up a pergola. One can always dream.

But while I watched this process unfold, God showed me something about dirt.

Once the old porch was torn down, we needed to fill our backyard with loads of dirt in order to raise the level of the ground for the walk-out patio. So one day, a man came to do just that. He climbed in a small Bobcat and sat in it for five or six hours, moving piles of dirt.

He drove slowly around in our backyard, filling his bucket with dirt from one pile and dumping it in another. He did this repeatedly. Then he would move the dirt again, pulling it back, pushing it forward, like he was icing an enormous cake. He made dozens of small, minute adjustments, over and over again.

He spent the whole day doing this. Hours and hours he worked, shifting soil around. As I watched him work slowly and steadily, from the dining room windows, I sympathized. Sometimes my life can feel like all I am doing is moving dirt from one spot to another.

I vacuum the same section of carpet day after day. I shuffle toys from the floor to a bin, over and over and over. I scrape spaghetti from pot to plate, and from plate to garbage can. (Did they even eat any?) Moving dirt. I hang up the same shirts, wipe the same fingerprints off the windows, and put the same books back on the same shelves. Moving dirt.

As I watched him through the windows, I thought about how boring moving dirt can be. It's not attractive work. It's not even the kind of work that shows a whole lot of progress. At the end of the day, our backyard was still covered in dirt. The man in the Bobcat didn't build a single thing. He never put a hammer to a nail on a fresh pine board or poured a drop of concrete. He just moved dirt. All. Day. Long.

But I was reminded the work he was doing was critical. And it is as much a part of the building process as pouring the cement or erecting a pergola. It is actually even more important because in order for the cement to be poured and the building of the patio to begin, the earth needs to be level and solid. He scraped and he pulled and he pushed until it was. He was building a solid foundation.

Motherhood is like sitting in a Bobcat leveling the ground, going back and forth over the same spot. Repeatedly. Moving a bucketful here, pulling a mound over there. Leveling the soil. Day after day, we don't see a lot of progress. The days are long and the years are short, as they say. Our workload can feel boring and repetitive because sometimes it is. But that doesn't make it any less important. The things we do are so much more than just pushing soil around, even though most days, it doesn't seem like it.

Responding to the cries in the middle of the night. Swathing antibacterial ointment on an owie. Rocking babies to sleep. Folding tiny socks and sweeping tiny crumbs. Making pizza on Friday night. Singing at the top of your lungs as you drive them to school. Hugs. Cards. Family dinners. Family devotions.

All the things we do—all the things—even the seemingly insignificant ones we did today, are building a bedrock of love and goodness for our children. We are laying a foundation. A solid foundation for our children to build upon. While driving them to Target, church, and preschool, we are modeling life to them, whether or not we realize it. We model love, forgiveness, goodness, safety, risk, patience, how to make mistakes, and how to persevere.

Zechariah 4:10 says, "Who dares despise the day of small things?" As a mother ,I love this verse because I, and probably you, are in that place. The place of small things. I also love this verse because it awakens again the idea that every great undertaking, whether it be painting a mural, curing cancer, mothering children, or building a patio, starts small. Starts ordinary. Starts with one good decision, day after day.

I love that we serve a God to whom every thing, no matter how small, matters a great deal. He never looks down on the small things, or small beginnings, because to Him, little things are sometimes the biggest in the upside-down Kingdom of God.

We may be in the day of small things, but this day is a gift, to us and to the children we are raising.

Friend, don't get down on the dirt. Don't get down on the fact that the job God has given you right now feels mundane, repetitive, and sometimes fruitless. Because it's not.

"Let us not become weary in doing good, for at the proper time we will reap a harvest if we do not give up" (Galatians 6:9).

Like the man in the Bobcat, we may never put a hammer to a nail, but our work is just as important.

Friend, what you are doing is worth it. The way you sacrifice, the way you sweep, the way you rock and pray, are helping to build a foundation for your children they will never forget. One upon which they will build for the rest of their lives. And that is no small thing. For God, for you, or for those little sticky-faced gifts of God you've been given.

PRAYER

Dear Lord, thank You for using Bobcats and dirt and construction workers to show us simple things about building a foundation. Foundational work may not look exciting, but it is oh so important. Remind us of this fact daily as we get bogged down in the ordinary work of motherhood and forget what we are ultimately building: lives. Lead us, Lord, as we raise these children, as we make a casserole and mop the floor, doing it all in the name of love. Remind us of the purpose of it all and give us strength to carry out the tasks before us. Let us not become weary in these things, knowing that if we do not give up, if we keep persevering, we will gain a reward for our work. In Your name, we pray. Amen.

Not Enough

"As a father has compassion on his children, so the LORD has compassion on those who fear him; for he knows how we are formed, he remembers that we are dust." Psalm 103:13–14

I sat on our bed and cried. My husband lay on his stomach in front of me, looking up with searching eyes. I blew my nose into a tissue. We had just been talking for the hundredth time this year about the fact that we are both running on empty. Overwhelmed with all that is on our plates, and a little unsure of what to do about it.

Sometimes in marriage when one is down, the other can help him up. But what happens when you're both overwhelmed? This was one of those seasons. And we were struggling to keep sane.

My husband is a self-employed business owner, has a growing heart for ministry in Rwanda and a role that goes with it, is a very involved father and husband, and has a lot of items on his "honey-do" list. Then there's me, trying to carve out time to write, following the call God has placed on my heart, doing ministry, and spending the bulk of my days taking care of our five wonderful, loving, energetic but sometimes exhausting children.

Then we moved to a ranch. A ranch that isn't a working one, but filled with work nonetheless. Fixing up our house, taking care of the few animals we have, and in springtime, mowing the acres and acres of grass around our house so we can spot a rattlesnake. Yes, you already know, our hands are full.

My husband looked up at me with his big honest blue eyes and said slowly, lovingly, hoping it would sink in, "You—are—not—enough. You don't have enough to give to these kids. We need help."

Tears came even quicker and I was full on sobbing into my Kleenex. He was right. His words weren't wounding. They were true. He wasn't calling me a bad mom or a neglectful one; he wasn't saying I wasn't capable or smart, or loving and kind. In fact, he often tells me what a great mother I am. But today, he was telling me what I already knew, and that was I simply didn't have enough to give. He was absolutely right.

I was trying to fill five little cups of water with an empty pitcher. Sometimes our cups runneth over, but what I've found—as a busy mom of young children—is that more often than not, my cup runneth dry. And I need help. While it feels like failure to admit it, it isn't. It is just reality.

I recently told a friend that I haven't cried a lot lately. That was a mistake. It was shortly after I said that, that the tears began. And they didn't stop. They came for all reasons, at all different moments, seemingly unconnected. I started to wonder what was happening to me. Was I depressed? Was I lonely? Was country life getting to me?

But as I sat on our bed that night, I realized it all boiled down to one thing: my cup was dry. Bone dry. I was overwhelmed by my responsibilities as a wife, mother, friend, housecleaner, organizer, appointment keeper, writer, driver, grocery-shopper, dinner-maker, laundry-doer, and homework helper.

As much as I tried, I couldn't seem to get it all done, and if I ever miraculously did, there was not an ounce of joy in it.

Perhaps the worst part was I was in denial. I kept fighting the overwhelming feelings of chaos and kids and running myself ragged, clenching my fists, determined that there had to be a way to get everything done and be in good spirits.

But the strain was evident. Evident in our marriage, evident in my reaction to the kids' behavior, evident in my own view of myself and feelings of inadequacy. I was constantly feeling under water without a ledge to hold on to. I felt like I wasn't enough.

That night, as we lay on the bed and I sobbed, I realized not only did I not feel like I was enough, I actually wasn't enough. It was a turning point, and I shed a lot of tears about a truth I already knew but had been denying. When I finally admitted it, it was life-giving.

The simple truth is that on my own, I am not enough. And I was suddenly so grateful that one of the names of our God is Savior. Savior. He saves us because we can't save ourselves.

Saves us from what exactly? Everything. From death and darkness. From fears and desperation. From the idea that we are somehow "good enough" on our own.

Some people try and tell us that we are enough, and we are the perfect mom for our kids. Yes, God definitely chose us to be the mothers of our children, but we in ourselves, fall so desperately short of being enough it isn't even funny.

I find much more encouragement in knowing that I wasn't made to be enough, than in trying to believe that in and of myself, I am. Because let's face it, this world is more than we can handle on our own. That's why we need Jesus. That's why He came to our rescue. He knows we are not enough. He came to do what we were powerless to do. He knows how weak we are. He knows, better than anyone in the universe, our unique limits.

And when we let go of the burden of perfection or being enough, it's like a whale was lifted off our shoulders.

God is not a pull-yourself-up-by-your-bootstraps kind of God. He is a God who picks us up, dusts us off, and calls us His own. Not because we worked hard for it, but because He did and we accepted His work on our behalf. He gives us things we didn't earn, takes us places we shouldn't be able to go, and does things for us we don't deserve.

Friend, if you're feeling overwhelmed like me, but a little defensive about it, I understand. And I would reach across the page and hug you if I could. And share my Kleenex. Not a used one, of course, that would be gross. But you could pull one from my box.

Then I would steal my husband's words and say, "You are not enough." And I would add, "But you weren't meant to be."

God loves you. He isn't surprised at your feelings of inadequacy. He isn't turned off by the fact that you can't do it all on your own. He already knows that. He made you that way. He made you to be in relationship with Him, the only One who is enough. He's ready and willing to help.

All you have to do is ask.

PRAYER

Lord, it's a funny thing to say, but thank You for making me "not enough." Thank You for making me with the need of a Savior. And thank You for being the One. I get so overwhelmed at times because I think it all relies on my strength and capabilities, but it's a relief to remember it doesn't. Hallalujah! So, God, come in and take over. Help us where we are weak. Come in and fill our souls with Your holy presence. Save us from ourselves and our own "good enough" thinking. Bring us from a kingdom of darkness into a kingdom of light (Colossians 1:13). The kingdom of Jesus Christ, the only One who is and always will be—enough. In His name, we pray. Amen.

When You Feel Unlovely

*"Long ago the L*ORD *said to Israel: 'I have loved you,
my people, with an everlasting love. With unfailing love
I have drawn you to myself.'" Jeremiah 31:3 NLT*

I remember exactly where I stood the first time I felt it. I was standing in the upstairs hallway of the first home we ever purchased, in the doorway of the only bathroom between our room on the left and my son's on the right. Yesterday's mascara clung to the dark circles underneath my eyes. I was wearing yoga pants and the T-shirt I went to bed in. It was way past the usual hour of dressing for the day, and I can't remember how long it had been since I showered. I had given birth a few weeks ago to our second son, and now had two babies under fourteen months of age.

I was grumpy, hormonal, and sleep deprived; all those things moms of newborns feel four weeks post-delivery. And I don't exactly know why, but I must have said something unkind out of my grumpiness because this awful feeling snuck up and surprised me. The feeling of being unlovely. I felt it, all over.

There have been times when I have felt put together on the outside but struggling within. Times when my hair was dried and my lip gloss was on, but I felt jealous or angry or unsure of myself. But this time, I felt all those things on the inside, in pajama pants and a spit-up covered T-shirt.

Until this moment, I had never felt so ugly—on the inside and the outside. And in times like these, when you don't even want to be around yourself, it's hard to imagine anyone else wanting to. When you don't like yourself, it seems like no one else could either.

And I wish I knew that day, that even when I feel unlovable, Jesus still loves me. You see, I knew Jesus. I believed in Him, but I often let my feelings of inadequacy overtake the reality of His love for me.

I needed that reminder then, and I need it today, because I am quick to forget. Maybe you are too. And maybe today, as you sit here with bedhead and in last night's T-shirt, you need to hear that you are loved in this moment, just as you are. Even if you've yelled at someone or said something you shouldn't have. Even if you haven't brushed your teeth.

We don't have to be lovely to be loved. We don't have to feel lovely, to be loved. We just are. Because God is. And He is love (1 John 4:8).

Recently I was reading in *The Jesus Storybook Bible* with my kids and we came across the story of the hidden treasure in Matthew 13:44. I had always seen this parable as Jesus telling us that the Kingdom of God is the treasure buried in a field, and we should give all we have to buy the field and essentially secure the Kingdom. But that wonderful little children's Bible illuminated something I had never seen before. Instead of it only being a lesson on the kind of desire we should have for the Kingdom of God, it pointed out that this is exactly what Jesus has done for us.

We are the treasure that was buried in the field. His treasure. And He sought us out, sold everything He had to buy the field with the treasure and rejoiced!

What the man in the parable did with the treasure, Jesus has done for us.

He gave up heaven for us. He gave up His very life for us. So that we would be His forever. Now that is what the Kingdom of God is like.

Romans 5:8 says, "God demonstrates his own love for us in this: While we were still sinners, Christ died for us."

While we were un-showered and wearing spit-up stained T-shirts, while we had mascara under our eyes and less than edifying words under our breath, our great God was loving us so much He was sending His Son to make a way for us to be with Him forever. To buy us back from the muck we find ourselves in. To pay a price we never could afford. Not because we looked nice or deserved it. Not because we were pretty or popular or always said kind things. But because we are His treasure. It is worth knowing our worth.

If today or tomorrow or someday, you find yourself feeling unlovely and unlovable, remember that you aren't. When you were at your worst, God sent His Best to find you, call you and redeem you, because—He loves you. You are loved. And lovely. And loveable. All those things. Why? Because we have One indescribable Father in heaven. There is no other reasonable explanation.

PRAYER

O Lord God, thank You for Your great love! What we sometimes see as a frumpy grumpy mom, somehow You still see as buried treasure. A gem. A pearl. We can never fully understand it, but as much as we are able, fill our hearts and our heads with understanding of how dearly and fiercely we are loved. For no other reason than You. Are. Love. Sometimes we feel so unworthy of it (and we are), and yet, You call us Your bride and Your treasure. Thank *You* for leaving Your throne in heaven, giving up everything You had because You believed finding and rescuing us was worth the cost. That is what Your kingdom is like. That is true love. And that is a God worth following. Hallelujah, we will be Yours forever! Amen.

Help Me Help Myself

"Because you are my helper, I sing for joy in the shadow of your wings" Psalm 63:7 NLT

One morning, I was helping my two-year-old daughter get dressed. But like many two-year-olds, she didn't want help. I know this is a good thing. It's also slightly annoying. I want my girls to become independent people who can and will do things for themselves. But…they're still two, and sometimes, they need help.

So I sat on the floor waiting to help as I watched her struggle to get her arms through her shirt. I gave her directions sitting cross-cross-applesauce holding back the urge to shove her arms through the holes. "Turn it this way. No, the other way. Too far—oops, it's backwards…" Finally, I couldn't take it anymore and I reached out to help.

She shrunk back and cried, "No! Help me, help myself!" and stomped her chubby little bare foot. She was determined; she wanted to do it. And I had to laugh at her words because of how I can relate. Just—let—me—do—it.

"Help me, help myself!"

But how does one truly help another help themselves? Isn't that kind of like an oxymoron? Doesn't it contradict itself? The very idea that you need help to help yourself, means simply you need help. Right? Not to mention the fact that whoever is saying this phrase, doesn't really want the help in the first place.

Sometimes that is kind of like my prayer life. I'm not sure if I really want Your help, God. I just want to do what I want to do, so if You could give me a little more time, or patience, energy, or whatever, then maybe,just maybe, I could do all the things I want, have all the patience, and I'd be good.

I stand there like a cute little ridiculous two-year-old struggling to stuff my arms through my shirt, while God sits patiently and offers assistance—offers to do what I am incapable of doing: putting on a shirt correctly.

Without realizing it, my life with God can turn into asking Him to help me become more and more independent, with less of a need for Him. But God's goal is never that I, or you, should need Him less. His goal is for us to know Him, love Him, glorify Him, and enjoy Him forever. Most of the time, that means we need to need Him more, not less.

Enter motherhood. Nothing has brought me to my knees quite like it. Many times, my hands have been overwhelmingly full and my insides completely empty.

There's that really sweet quote, I am sure you know it well. "If you think my hands are full, you should see my heart." So great. But if I am being honest, more often than not, for me that heart is not full of the blessings of childrearing, it is drained by it.

Sometimes, I forget to look at my children and smile. I forget to see them as gifts and instead feel them as burdens. I stare at the hard and overlook the good.

Because while I wanted nothing more in life than to be a mother (and write) it has challenged me in ways I never imagined.

I never imagined my body carrying and nursing twins. I never imagined five kids. I never imagined them so close together. I never, I never, I never.

But God did. Twins and five kids in six years was always part of God's plan for me and for our family. Twins may have been a shock to me but they were not a shock to God, a wise woman once told me as I sat pouring my heart out to her, tears and snot mixing together and running down my nose.

I thought perhaps, if I had had less kids, or had them farther apart, I could have done this with ease and even remembered to be the tooth fairy. I could have done this whole mom thing according to my own natural ability. I am now smart enough to realize that isn't true. No kids or ten kids, we all need Jesus like fruit flies need a banana.

Still, these five little energetic blessings have been God's way of reminding me time and time again, "apart from me, you can do nothing" (John 15:5).

Truer words were never spoken. In my own strength, I'm fairly useless. I need lots of help.

Psalm 63:7 says, "because you are my helper, I sing for joy in the shadow of your wings" (NLT). When I realize I can't, neither was I meant to, do this on my own, I am relieved. He is my helper—and oh how I need one.

Psalm 46:1 calls God an "ever-present help in trouble." Ever-present. I love that. He never leaves us. Even when we push Him away, stomp our feet, and want to do it our own way, He sits and waits ready to help.

He uses motherhood, moving, loneliness, illness, earthquakes and fires—and a host of other things to draw us to Himself and remind us that apart from Him we can do nothing. He is the only One with the power to transform lives and hearts. The only One who gives supernatural strength in super uncomfortable circumstances that come with life and motherhood. He stands ready to help.

Oh that we would receive it!

So, instead of asking Him for things I need to help me help myself, may I simply ask for help. May I call on the name of Jesus for my strength and look to Him in moments of weakness.

May I learn to surrender. May I learn to pray prayers of acceptance, prayers for His will, not mine. May you and I trust Him to be our Helper and stop trying to do it on our own so that we may live life in a way that brings Him glory. Because we were made to do just that.

PRAYER

Father, how we need You. We can do nothing without You. You hold all things together! We confess we have tried to do this life, this mom-thing on our own. But it isn't possible. Our own strength, might, patience, wit, and love just isn't enough. We come to You, not seeking Your help, so we can help ourselves, but seeking to be filled with Your Holy Spirit so that our lives would be an outpouring of all that is good and pure and holy. O God, come to our rescue and be our Helper. Be our Comforter, and our Prince of Peace. We are so thankful the government (and parenthood and all other things) rests on Your shoulders (Isaiah 9:6) not on ours. Thank You, Jesus! Help us today, to learn to lean on You, now and forevermore. Amen.

Acknowledgements

F irst of all, *God*. Without Him, I wouldn't be living or breathing. Definitely wouldn't be writing. And if not for Him, I would have never had the call, the courage, or strength to write this book.

Second, none of this would have been possible without the love, support, encouragement and belief of my husband, and the lives and inspiration of our wild and wonderful children. So, *Darrell, Jacob, Landon, Lee, Halle, and Ruthie*—this one's for you.

A SPECIAL THANKS

It takes a village to raise children and to write a book when you have small children. A special thanks to my sister *Heather*, herself a mother of five kids and a total mom boss, she read and reread these devotionals and gave such insightful advice it was like she was in my head. A very special thanks to my dear friends *Amy, Carrie, and Jessica B.* who graciously captured pictures of our hands full life and used their creative talents to create something beautiful. This book wouldn't be the same without you!

And many thanks to my friends and family who have given such support to me and my family along the way and continued to believe in what God was doing in me, especially when I didn't.

If you enjoyed this book, will you consider sharing it with others?

- Please mention the book on Facebook, Twitter, Pinterest, or your blog.
- Recommend this book to your small group, book club, and workplace.
- Head over to Facebook.com/CrossRiverMedia, 'Like' the page and post a comment as to what you enjoyed the most.
- Pick up a copy for someone you know who would be challenged or encouraged by this message.
- Write a review on Amazon.com, BN.com, or Goodreads.com.
- To learn about our latest releases subscribe to our newsletter at www.CrossRiverMedia.com.

About the Author

Brooke and her husband, Darrell, live the full life just outside of Sacramento California with their five blonde and energetic children.

Brooke loves Jesus, her family, and encouraging women, especially moms in the thick of it like herself. When she's not wiping dirt off anything white in her home or carting kids around, you can find her visiting with friends, trying to write, attempting to run, and avoiding laundry. Her dreams are big, her hands are full and, yes, her laundry room is a mess.

BrookeFrick.com
Instagram.com/brookellenfrick
Facebook.com/brookellenfrick

Abba's
ANSWERS

30 Stories of God's Answers to Prayer

More great devotionals from...
CROSSRIVERMEDIA.COM

THE BENEFIT PACKAGE

Love, redemption, mercy, provision, revelation and healing... In Psalm 103, David listed just a few of the good things God did for him. His list gives us plenty to be thankful for during tough times. No matter your circumstances or background, God is always full of compassion, generous with his mercy, unfailing in his love and powerful in healing. When circumstances overwhelm you — unwrap his *Benefit Package* and rediscover God's goodness.

UNBEATEN

Difficult times often leave Christians searching the Bible for answers to the most difficult questions — Does God hear me when I pray? Why isn't He doing anything? As author Lindsey Bell searched the Bible for answers to these tough questions. Her studies led her through the stories of biblical figures, big and small. She discovered that while life brings trials, faith brings victory. And when we rely on God for the strength to get us through, we can emerge *Unbeaten*.

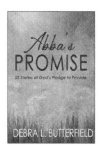

ABBA'S PROMISE

Start your day with a dose of faith. These true stories will cure your fear and doubts. In Abba's Promise, you'll find thirty-three personal stories of God's provision. Discover how God used purple socks, a steel pipe, and a corn maze to answer prayers. These inspiring stories will encourage you and strengthen your faith. If you like reading uplifting anthologies, you'll enjoy Abba's Promise.

Made in the USA
Coppell, TX
21 May 2022

78033026R00087